Digital Storyte

This innovative, accessible book is an introduction to using digital storytelling in language teaching, with a focus on English as an Additional Language (EAL) instruction. Linville and Vinogradova provide a clear framework that addresses translanguaging and multimodal meaning making in teaching multilingual learners (MLs) through the use of digital storytelling.

This book provides detailed guidance on how to incorporate digital storytelling into language teaching, building on recent developments in the fields of TESOL and language education that position multilingualism and multiliteracies as important components of any language instruction. Through this text and accompanying activities, readers will understand how to work with MLs to create multimodal digital texts. This book offers an easy-to-follow, step-by-step process for language educators to follow to support MLs' digital storytelling projects in any EAL classroom. Featured digital storytelling projects from EAL practitioners in various contexts, as well as multiple examples and resources, are included for each stage of the process, always grounded in contemporary TESOL theories (e.g., critical pedagogy, culturally responsive teaching, translanguaging, and a pedagogy of multiliteracies). This framework supports the development of multilingualism and multiliteracies and can be adapted by educators of other world languages for any language education setting.

Grounded in contemporary TESOL theories, this book is an essential text for courses on technology in TESOL and TESOL methods courses, as well as for language educators.

Heather A. Linville, PhD is Professor and Chair of Educational Studies at the University of Wisconsin, La Crosse, USA, where she teaches undergraduate teacher candidates to be knowledgeable, critical, and ethical teachers of multilingual learners.

Polina Vinogradova, PhD is Hurst Senior Professorial Lecturer and TESOL Program Director at American University in Washington, D.C., USA, where she works with undergraduate and graduate TESOL students.

To all teachers of multilingual learners who are working to raise up their multilingual voices.

Heather dedicates this book to her favorite coauthor, Polina, and to Todd, Carter, and Lingon, who put up with her, again, in the birthing of this book. All my love.

Polina dedicates this book to her daughter Mira Valentina, with whom she is now writing a new story in her life. У нас с тобой впереди так много интересных историй и приключений.

Contents

Featured Digital Storytelling Project Contributors

Fatima Aldajani contributed the featured digital storytelling project "Digital Stories with High School Refugee and Immigrant Students," in Chapter 3. She is an ESL Instructor at the American Language Institute at the University of Toledo in Ohio, USA.

Debora Amidani and **Carlye Stevens** both work at The Family Place Public Charter School in Washington, DC, USA. Debora is ESL Instructor and Carlye is Digital Literacy and Technology Instructor. Their project "Digital Stories with Adult Beginner Low Literacy English Language Learners" is featured in Chapter 5.

Nada Filipovic is an English Language Teacher and Teaching Advisor in the Sabacka gimnazija grammar school in Sabac, Serbia. Her featured digital storytelling project, "Social Issues—I am concerned about …" appears in Chapter 8.

Andrea Enikő Lypka contributed the featured digital storytelling project "Through Our Lens: Student Perspectives about Navigating Identities in Academia through Student-created Visual Texts," in Chapter 7. She is an English for Academic Purposes instructor at the University of South Florida in Tampa, Florida, USA.

Aimee Leisy shared the featured project, "That's My Story: A Public Speaking Event," in Chapter 10. Aimee is Assistant Teaching Professor in the Intensive English Program of the Department of English at Wichita State University in Wichita, Kansas, USA.

Nadezda Pimenova is Senior Lecturer at Purdue Language and Cultural Exchange (PLaCE) at Purdue University in West Lafayette, Indiana, USA. Her project "'Telling my Story': an EAP Bridge Course Project," is featured in Chapter 12.

Tamara Mae Roose is Assistant Professor of TESOL, Department of Teacher Education and Foundations, California State University, San Bernardino in California, USA. She wrote about her digital storytelling project, "Reflections on My Language and Culture Identity," while working at Mercy College in New York, USA. It appears in Chapter 6.

Dana Saito-Stehberger and **Clare Jimeno** collaborated on the featured digital storytelling project, "Elementary Computing for All" in Chapter 4. Dana is Director of Curriculum and Professional Development at the Digital Learning Lab at the University of California, Irvine. Clare is a fifth grade Gifted and Talented Education teacher at Muir Fundamental Elementary School in Santa Ana Unified School District. They are both located in California, USA.

Megan M. Siczek is Associate Professor of English for Academic Purposes (EAP) at George Washington University in Washington, DC, USA. Her digital storytelling project, "Telling My Own Language Story: Digital Literacy Narratives in the EAP Classroom" is featured in Chapter 9.

Vanessa Virgiel is a lecturer in the Department of English at the Korea Military Academy in Seoul, South Korea. Her featured project, "Digital Animation Project" is in Chapter 2.

Digital Stories

To access these stories as Support Material, please scan the QR code.

Events That Gave Me Confidence: https://www.youtube.com/watch?v=LaklSvtVwnA
Finding Home: https://youtu.be/GnKNWgOeowY
From Guatemala to the US: https://www.youtube.com/watch?v=lcYjs35fcKo&t=296s
A Good Hmong Woman: https://www.youtube.com/watch?v=aOGYcDhxPgs
Here!: https://youtu.be/aavW3Tzt58c
Home: https://youtu.be/2eAT4X-Na84
Home Movies: https://www.youtube.com/watch?v=bKuGpBaWqQk
How I Become an ArmyBlink Girl in My Life: https://youtu.be/ppXrTlsDqGg
I am American, but …: https://www.youtube.com/watch?v=8LUZBhPjb8c
I Belong with Both: https://www.youtube.com/watch?v=YpjGwtoWfk4
Learning a New Language to Change My Future: https://www.youtube.com/watch?v=mFS2PhUGG2k&t=2s
Living the Dream: https://vimeo.com/265269480
Me and Military: https://youtu.be/MZkzO-pneXA
Mes Parents: https://www.youtube.com/watch?v=SCHqw3YPvO4&t=2s
My Big Foot: https://youtu.be/Jcsk2R8_esM
My Father https://youtu.be/JPeX7qRsC3E
My Story of Jing Di Zhi Wa: https://youtu.be/ILds0KnCTRI

Real Men Do Housework: https://www.youtube.com/watch?v=YT6cBfscybs&t=1s
Remaking El Rancho: https://www.youtube.com/watch?v=5IrKOS5jJao
Sacrificios: https://www.youtube.com/watch?v=QBf9syEsX4A
What Is Home?: https://www.youtube.com/watch?v=T8EMZTdW8XI
Who Am I as an English Language Teacher: https://vimeo.com/444992145

Illustrations

Figures

Tables

Preface

Digital storytelling is an engaging form of multimodal expression, useful and valuable for language educators and multilingual learners (MLs). It is economical, facilitates creative collaboration, improves upon students' various language and life skills, and encourages building communities of practice in language classrooms. We both started exploring and using digital stories in the early 2000s when Heather was working at the English Language Center and Polina was a PhD student and also working at the English Language Center at the University of Maryland, Baltimore County (UMBC). In that work, we both incorporated digital storytelling as final student projects in our content-based academic English courses—Higher Education in the US, Intercultural Communication, and New Media and Culture.

In this video recorded at UMBC in 2009, we talk about the value and benefits of using digital stories in English language education: https://www.youtube.com/watch?v=72aJ1G0acSE&t=9s.

When using digital storytelling projects in our classes, we observed various reactions from the MLs. At the beginning, many were puzzled by the project and assignments that came with it, while others were excited. Some MLs felt the project wasn't appropriate for a university class as they expected the teacher to be in front of the classroom lecturing and delivering knowledge as they digested and acquired this knowledge and then reproduced it back for a grade. Digital storytelling projects challenge and dismiss this banking approach to learning and teaching a language. Rather, they give the power of content choices to the MLs, emphasize creative meaning making, and put the teacher in the position of facilitator and guide.

The creative and collaborative process of digital story production also allows MLs to get to know each other in ways they often don't in the classroom. When the New London Group (2000) describes the four components of a pedagogy of multiliteracies, they talk about students' (including MLs') lifeworlds in connection with situated practice. By lifeworlds, they mean students' knowledge, experiences, interests, and various other aspects of their lives that they bring into the educational process. That is exactly what we observed in our classes—MLs were bringing their lifeworlds into the learning environment and their learning. The topics of their digital stories revealed important aspects of their lives, often joyous, but sometimes sad and traumatic. They told stories about their families; about life-defining events like becoming a parent, immigrating, or serving in the military; about navigating cultural differences; and how they have found the strength to do new things and overcome their fears, among other important topics. We observed MLs becoming vulnerable, shedding tears when listening to each other or watching each other's stories, and establishing friendships based on common interests and life experiences. They also argued over grammar and the clarity of their narratives. They communicated with their families and friends about their projects, seeking advice and asking for photos to be sent to them. Through our digital storytelling projects, we've observed the most skeptical MLs open up and produce powerful multimodal narratives.

> Watch the digital story *Mes Parents*; https://www.youtube.com/watch?v=SCHqw3YPvO4&t=2s. Notice how the author addresses his parents in the digital story. To a certain degree, he produced the digital story with his mother. He wrote the narrative in English, then translated it into French, sent it to his mother, and asked her to select and send him family photographs that she found appropriate. Most of the photographs we see in his digital story were selected by her. This digital story was produced in Polina's class in summer 2008.

After we both left UMBC and started working with pre-service teachers in TESOL education programs, we continued incorporating digital storytelling projects into our courses. In this work, we have seen a similar response—initial skepticism, excitement, vulnerability, and creativity. While some pre-service teachers struggle to express themselves multimodally, others embrace the genre and not only enthusiastically complete their digital stories, but also carry these projects forward, incorporating them into their own teaching. An example of this is the digital storytelling project featured in Chapter 5, carried out by Polina's former MA TESOL students Debora Amidani and Carlye Stevens.

This book is a result of many years of our collaboration where we researched advocacy, multimodality, and empowerment of MLs and language educators. In this work, we see close connections between digital storytelling and advocacy as digital stories create a multimodal space to express diverse multilingual voices. We also see it as a tool for teachers and others to advocate for linguistic justice. In this book, we want to show how MLs' rich and diverse linguistic repertoires can be incorporated into the language learning process. Thus, we write this book with a translanguaging stance and show how translanguaging and digital storytelling can be purposefully present in a language classroom. While we focus on English as an additional language in educational settings, we believe that our perspective on digital storytelling projects and this book will be useful to any language educator.

We also want this book to be a practical step-by-step guide for language teachers, one that will guide you from envisioning and planning the digital storytelling project, through the steps in its implementation, to project evaluation and assessment. We hope that language teachers around the world will find the worksheets, materials, and resources we have included useful.

For us this book represents almost two decades of personal friendship and academic collaboration. We welcome you to this journey and hope you find it as exciting and fruitful as we have!

Reference

New London Group. (2000). A pedagogy of multiliteracies designing social futures. In B. Cope & M. Kalantzis (Eds.), *Multiliteracies: Literacy learning and the design of social futures* (pp. 9–37). Routledge. https://doi.org/10.17763/haer.66.1.17370n67v22j160u

Acknowledgements

Our most heartfelt appreciation to Beverly (Bev) Bickel and Bill Shewbridge at the University of Maryland, Baltimore County (UMBC) who had the foresight and vision to bring digital storytelling to UMBC and the English Language Center over 15 years ago. In 2005, Polina took Bill's class on digital media and produced her first digital story, which put her on the path of digital storytelling exploration. In 2007, Bev encouraged Heather and Polina to work together and bring digital stories to the English Language Center where they both worked. We also thank Joe Lambert for his pioneering work and support all these years.

Thank you, also, to all our students throughout the years who have allowed us to enjoy creating digital stories with them and analyze how they did it. Thank you for your perseverance, hard work, wonderful creativity, and feedback on our ideas. You inspire us every day.

Finally, we thank Lisa Lenarz for her beautiful art work and design of the cover of the book and Safa Qureshi for her excellent support in editing and formatting this book.

Polina thanks her amazing coauthor Heather for joining her in this digital storytelling journey. Thank you for your friendship and for making this work a great joy. She also thanks her husband Ayhan for his never-ending love, support of all of her endeavors, and for exciting adventures over the years.

Heather thanks her parents, Larry and Martha Linville, for inspiring storytelling from the beginning.

Work on this book was supported by the Faculty Mellon Fund from the College of Arts & Sciences at American University.

Acronyms and Abbreviations

CoP	community of practice
EAL	English as an additional language
EAP	English for academic purposes
EFL	English as a foreign language
ESL	English as a second language
MLs	multilingual learners
TESOL	teaching English to speakers of other languages

Part I Setting the Stage

1 Introduction

Storytelling is an essential human activity. Through storytelling, we make connections, share who we are, and learn about others. As Barkhuizen (2018) notes,

> It is often claimed that in the act of storytelling people make meaning of their lives. In the process of constructing and narrating a story they interpret life events by establishing patterns of coherence among them. Exposure to stories narrated by others prompts reflection on one's own life and, importantly for the classroom, stimulates the imagination and generates interest in and knowledge about the lives of others.
>
> (p. 1)

Everyone has a story to tell. Language learners everywhere, who we refer to as multilingual learners (MLs) throughout this book, need to share their experiences with each other to tell their stories in their multiple languages. Second language acquisition theories, such as sociocultural theory, interaction theory, and input and output theories, tell us that MLs need opportunities to speak and write, as well as read and listen, and need opportunities to do so with others. They also need to communicate about ideas and concepts that are personally meaningful (Dörnyei & Ushioda, 2021) and have the space to negotiate and express their identities (Norton, 2013). Storytelling is the perfect activity to meet those needs. Digital storytelling, a modern version of storytelling, is an interactive, engaging, and creative way to bring students' stories into the classroom.

Watch this digital story by a university-level ML and consider the creator's agency and power as a storyteller: *My Big Foot*; https://youtu.be/Jcsk2R8_esM. Think about the story you want to tell and the decisions you would make about what elements to include. This digital story was produced in Heather's class in fall 2008.

DOI: 10.4324/9781003295730-2

Purpose of This Book

This book is a guide to digital storytelling with MLs. We believe that digital storytelling can be very useful and powerful in language classrooms for multiple reasons. The digital storytelling process is creative and personally meaningful to learners as they choose each element, word, image, and music to include in their story. Importantly, ML creators have final decision-making power over each element of their story. Every step is taken to express who the creators are and to reflect on their lives.

The digital storytelling process is also one of collaboration and provides many opportunities for language learning. Learners interact with each other and teachers through conversations, questions, and peer review. They negotiate meaning and develop language skills as they produce the digital story that best tells their story. The digital storytelling process develops ML agency and empowers them as language learners as they make decisions about language use at each stage of the digital storytelling process. MLs build their knowledge of each aspect of language, making choices about the vocabulary, grammatical structures, and discourse styles to use to best express their story's meaning. Digital stories produced in the classroom can also create an environment of trust as learners and teachers establish connections and learn about each other through the sharing of their stories.

Digital storytelling can be a tool for social justice. MLs' digital stories can be shared outside the classroom, highlighting and raising awareness of their unique experiences and perspectives. Digital stories are especially engaging to audiences because they are multimodal and can be viewed by one or a million people at the same time and in multiple locations.

> Watch this digital story created by a high-school migrant to get a sense of the power of stories in a digital format: *Finding Home*; https://youtu.be/GnKNWgOeowY. Think if you were to produce your own digital story, what would be some of the ideas you would want to share? This story was produced in Heather and Polina's workshop in summer 2022.

This book is also a guide on how to use digital storytelling as translanguaging. MLs come to our classrooms speaking multiple languages and often engage in translanguaging, using their full linguistic repertoire. Digital storytelling is a way to value all languages and the ways MLs use them, and to support MLs as they learn to navigate communities that are more or less multilingual. While producing digital stories in English, creators can use their multiple languages and rely on their multilingual repertoires to develop messages that are accessible to a wider audience, including family and friends. Through digital storytelling, we can encourage MLs to translanguage, to share their stories in the most authentic way possible. Language barriers do not exist because images, music, the voiceover, various special effects, and subtitles can convey the meaning of the story.

Digital storytelling with translanguaging can also be a tool for linguistic justice as creators use language as they choose to tell their story in the most authentic and personally meaningful way possible. As translanguaged digital stories are shared beyond the classroom, audiences learn and understand more of the linguistic diversity of MLs in their communities. In this book, we also highlight the ways digital storytelling with translanguaging can improve educational and social equity for MLs.

Watch this digital story by a university-level ML to see translanguaging in action: *My Father*; https://youtu.be/JPeX7qRsC3E. Think about the language(s) you would use to tell your story. When would you use other languages besides English? When would you use a variety of English not taught in schools? This digital story was produced in Polina's class in summer 2008.

Finally, this book is a guide for teachers that shows how to prepare, plan, and incorporate translanguaging and digital storytelling into their teaching. It guides language educators through the step-by-step process of how to create digital stories, tailored specifically for working with language learners and with a translanguaging, multilingual lens. This engagement with multimodal content and multiple languages can support MLs' language learning through their creative engagement and deep personal connections. At the same time, it requires carefully thought-out and planned methodology and flexibility on the part of the teacher. We include activities that can be used in your language classroom to reach these goals.

With this book, our goals are to:

1. Explain why and how digital storytelling is useful in language teaching;
2. Provide a clear, step-by-step process for creating digital stories in the language classroom;
3. Connect digital storytelling to the goals of translanguaging so it can be more easily understood and incorporated into language teaching; and
4. Provide multiple examples and resources to support digital storytelling creation with translanguaging in any language classroom.

Please note, most of our examples in the book focus on MLs, students who are learning English as an additional language in classrooms around the globe. However, digital storytelling is a valuable pedagogical tool in any language classroom. We also want to note that the book format requires us to structure this work in a linear way. But digital storytelling work in language education—being multimodal and dependent on many factors, including MLs' language proficiency, overall literacy and technological literacy levels, curricular goals, and so on—needs to be flexible. In some contexts, you might choose to start the project by brainstorming and then writing a verbal narrative (e.g., in academic writing classes), but in other settings, starting with brainstorming and selecting visuals or talking about music that creates a certain mood and message might be more useful and productive. We encourage you to interpret our suggested project stages with this flexibility in mind and tailor them to your MLs' needs and curricular demands. At the same time, we cannot emphasize enough the value and need for advanced planning and preparation to ensure the success of your digital storytelling project with your MLs.

Organization of the Book

Throughout the book, we highlight digital storytelling projects from English language teachers in a variety of teaching contexts around the globe. These projects provide concrete examples of the variety of ways digital storytelling with translanguaging can be implemented.

In Part I, we set the stage for digital storytelling in the language classroom. In Chapter 2, we inform the reader about the history of digital storytelling as well as current practices. We also provide an overview of the steps of digital storytelling as related to translanguaging, orienting the reader to the organization of the book. In Chapter 3, we explore the theoretical underpinnings of this work, providing a strong foundation for the rest of the book.

In Part II, we discuss each step of the digital storytelling process in detail with examples, resources, and sample materials. Chapter 4 helps teachers be well prepared for digital storytelling, setting up their classroom and curriculum for success. Chapter 5 explains how to best prepare MLs for a successful digital storytelling project. Chapter 6 describes the first step in digital storytelling, the story circle, and includes activities and examples from story circles we have conducted with a variety of MLs. Chapter 7 provides details on how to support MLs as they choose, create, or prepare the multimodal components of their digital story—the voiceover, images, and background music. In this chapter, we also explain how to support MLs as they arrange and rearrange each of the components to best tell their story, with guidance for common issues. In Chapter 8, we focus on the final stages of digital storytelling—video editing and multimodal composing—to create the strongest and most compelling authentic story for each creator. In Chapter 9, we discuss how peer collaboration and feedback support all stages of digital storytelling and foster a classroom culture of storytellers and creators working together. Finally, in Chapter 10, we review various options for presenting and sharing MLs' digital stories, with considerations of the advantages and disadvantages of each option.

In Part III, in Chapter 11, we guide readers through a reflection on evaluation and assessment of digital stories. We include examples of rubrics which consider the trickier elements of assessment of creative works. We delve into a discussion of the ways digital storytelling can be used for advocacy and empowerment for MLs and community building among multilingual creators and monolingual audience members. In Chapter 12, we revisit the theoretical foundations of digital storytelling and situate digital story creation more firmly in Teaching English to Speakers of Other Languages (TESOL) multilingual theories.

> Watch this digital story and consider how the creator, who was a TESOL teacher candidate when making this digital story, can relate to her English language learners: *Living the Dream*; https://vimeo.com/265269480. This digital story was produced in Polina's class in spring 2016.

In Conclusion

This book is written for anyone in the field of TESOL or involved in any language teaching. We wrote it for practitioners, those who are currently teaching MLs. We know teachers worry about their own digital expertise, getting buy-in from administrators, or the time commitment needed to take on a digital storytelling project. We feature throughout the book several digital storytelling projects from real language teachers with real MLs to demonstrate how to create your own digital storytelling project and overcome challenges that may arise. The multiple examples and resources we include are grounded in contemporary TESOL theories and can also be adapted by educators of other world languages for any language teaching context. We hope you will continually rely on this book as a reference in your classroom as you and your MLs produce digital stories. We also hope that teacher educators will use this book as a guide to prepare future teachers to use digital storytelling in their classrooms. We imagine it will serve as a reference for scholars and researchers interested in translanguaging, multimodality and personal narratives, and multilingualism. If you are not using digital storytelling yet with your MLs, we hope you will be soon!

References

Barkhuizen, G. (2018). Storytelling. In J. I. Liontas (Ed.), *The TESOL encyclopedia of English language teaching*. https://doi.org/10.1002/9781118784235.eelt0184

Dörnyei, Z. & Ushioda, E. (2021). *Teaching and researching motivation*, 3rd edition. Taylor and Francis. https://doi.org/10.4324/9781351006743

Norton, B. (2013). *Identity and language learning: Extending the conversation*, 2nd edition. De Gruyter. https://doi.org/10.21832/9781783090563

2 The History and Practice of Digital Storytelling

> In October of 2008, Heather's academic English language class for international MLs at the University of Maryland, Baltimore County (UMBC) in the United States was bubbling with ideas and suggestions. They had just begun working on their digital stories, a project introduced to them by Polina. The MLs were working in groups discussing ideas for their digital stories, giving each other advice, arguing about some points and agreeing on others. We, as instructor (Heather) and researcher (Polina), were sitting at times and walking around at other times observing. The MLs didn't seem to notice us, they didn't seem to need us. They were fully engaged in their story circle activity, arranged in four groups of six, with an ML leader in each group. All MLs were asked to think of ideas for their digital stories—themes and topics, types of images, types of music, main messages of their stories, and who they wanted to watch their stories. The conversations were involved, and when they deviated from the topics, the leaders carefully brought them back on track. The groups were linguistically diverse, including Arabic, French, German, Korean, Mandarin Chinese, and Russian speakers, with about half of the MLs being Korean speakers. The conversation was predominantly in English, with some elements of translanguaging, mostly brief clarifications that happened in languages other than English. The MLs were all busy and looked happy; they were working and they were interested.

This short vignette of our first collaborative experience with digital storytelling in a language classroom highlights why we were first inspired by the engagement, creativity, multimodality, multilingualism, collaboration, empowerment, and self-expression of digital storytelling. Since that first experience, we have incorporated digital stories in our teaching, designing courses that revolve around multilingualism and digital storytelling. In this chapter, we look in detail at what digital stories are and describe the history of the digital storytelling movement. We also provide an overview of the collaborative steps of digital storytelling which will each be explored in more detail in subsequent chapters.

Digital Stories

Digital storytelling has rapidly developed since the first digital storytelling workshop at the American Film Institute in 1993. It is now an interactive

DOI: 10.4324/9781003295730-3

community of practice including digital story enthusiasts, educators, and scholars. Most follow the model of the StoryCenter (www.storycenter.org), which allows for creator control over every aspect of production as a form of democratization that empowers creators. In this unique nonlinear multimodal narrative genre, storytellers utilize new media technology to produce short personal narratives using sound and images. As Hartley and McWilliam (2009) put it, digital storytelling "combines the direct emotional charge of confessional disclosure, the authenticity of the documentary, and the simple elegance of the format – it is a digital sonnet, or haiku" (p. 5).

Digital stories are short (two- to five-minute) personal, and often autobiographical, narratives. They are stories in that they have a clear storyline and dramatic storytelling qualities and can include impressionistic and poetic expressions. They are digital in that they combine verbal narration (the narrative voiceover) with visual images and musical background and can be produced using commonly available video editing software (e.g., Final Cut Pro, i-Movie, PowerDirector, WeVideo, etc.). Digital stories can also include various special effects, animation, mash-ups of videos and still images, and added text in various forms. Narrative expression can include chronological narratives, poetry, travelogs, and autobiographies to name a few.

One crucial aspect of digital storytelling is that a digital story is a personal multimodal narrative. Lambert (2009) and Lambert and Hessler (2018) emphasize that these multimodal narratives have their own place among other pieces of information produced with the use of new media technology due to their narrative quality and a potential for creators to develop and convey powerful messages using symbolic means. The creators of digital stories use multimodality to express themselves as storytellers while reflecting on important and often crucial and life-changing experiences. They explore connections among people, events, and places and develop connections between the author, their story, and the audience while establishing a multidimensional and multimodal dialogue.

This multimodal power of digital stories, which calls for engagement with the audience, includes seven elements (Lambert, 2006):

1. the point of view of the creator;
2. a dramatic question that "set[s] up a tension" (p. 50) and captivates the audience throughout the story;
3. the emotional content in the digital story;
4. the presence of the creator's voice which adds to the emotional content of the digital story and allows the creator to emphasize different elements of the narrative;
5. the soundtrack or musical background which also convey emotions and create emphasis;

6. economy of expression, meaning the creator effectively uses multimodality to convey meaning without overstating the message of their digital story; and
7. pacing, which refers to the flow and speed of the digital story, that does not feel too slow or too fast.

We find the preceding list useful as it helps us guide MLs in the creation of their stories. Later, Lambert (2009) redefined these elements and reformulated them as seven suggestions for the process of digital storytelling as follows:

1. owning one's insights as a creator;
2. owning the emotional side of the story in order to connect more deeply to the audience;
3. finding the moment of change in the story;
4. seeing the story through visual imagery, both explicit and implicit;
5. hearing the story and setting the tone;
6. assembling the story, keeping in mind the audience's needs and reactions; and
7. sharing the digital story with an audience.

We will return to both of these lists, especially when we think about the assessment of digital stories in Chapter 11. Keeping these collaborative, multimodal elements in mind, we now look at the history of digital storytelling as a global movement to empower storytellers.

Digital Storytelling Movement

Dana Atchley is considered to be the grandfather of the digital storytelling movement (see Hartley & McWilliam, 2009; Lambert, 2009; Lambert & Hessler, 2018). In his show, *Next Exit*, Atchley told his own personal stories while playing music and showing family videos and photographs on the screen. This combination of personal oral narratives, visuals of various formats, and music was the beginning of the digital storytelling genre.

> Watch Atchley's digital story *Home Movies* here: https://www.youtube.com/watch?v=bKuGpBaWqQk.

In 1994, Dana Atchley, Joe Lambert, and Nina Mullen founded the San Francisco Digital Media Center, which later moved to Berkeley, CA and became the Center for Digital Storytelling (https://www.storycenter.org/history). Now known as the StoryCenter (http://www.storycenter.org), it offers a variety of digital storytelling workshops and programs and is a great resource for digital storytelling.

> Check out StoryCenter's rich collection of digital stories produced in their workshops and programs over the years (https://www.youtube.com/c/StoryCenter), including the story that inspired Polina's journey in digital storytelling: *Sacrificios* by Ernesto Ayala; https://www.youtube.com/watch?v=QBf9syEsX4A).

Festivals and conferences dedicated to digital storytelling occur annually and bring together creators, producers, and researchers working on various aspects of the genre. For example, together with the Museum of the Person International Network (Brazil, Canada, Portugal, and US; https://www.comminit.com/content/museum-person-global-network-life-stories), the StoryCenter designated May 16 as the International Day for Sharing Life Stories, calling on people to gather at universities, schools, community centers, and other public places to share their digital stories. Until 2005, the Digital Storytelling Festival annually brought together authors, producers, and people interested in the movement. Further, digital storytellers from around the world meet annually at the International Conference on Digital Storytelling in various locations around the world (http://stories.umbc.edu/index.php/past-conferences/).

> Examples of community-based digital storytelling projects:
>
> - *Stories of Service* (a project devoted to the stories of veterans run by the Digital Clubhouse Network in San Jose, CA)
> - *German Immigration into the U.S.* (UMBC, http://www.umbc.edu/blogs/digitalstories/2009/12/digital_stories_from_german_30.html)
> - *Outta Your Backpack* (Indigenous Action Media, Flagstaff, AZ; https://indigenousaction.org/backpack/about.html)
> - *Digital Underground Storytelling for Youth* (DUSTY) (a literacy project for inner-city youth in Oakland, CA; Nelson & Hull, 2008)
> - *Silence Speaks* (http://www.silencespeaks.org/)
> - *Stories for Change* (http://storiesforchange.net/)

Digital storytelling programs are mostly run by educational and cultural institutions, community centers and organizations, and various government, business, and religious organizations and focus on historical, aspirational, and recuperative themes (McWilliam, 2009). Influenced and often in collaboration with the StoryCenter, several universities established digital storytelling programs and initiatives, created online collections of digital stories and educational materials, and have been supporting faculty and students as they incorporate digital stories into academic curricula. In particular, the University of Maryland, Baltimore County (UMBC), where we started our work with digital stories, keeps a rich archive of digital stories produced by English language learners.

Explore digital storytelling resources, projects, and collections at universities:

- The University of Houston: https://digitalstorytelling.coe.uh.edu
- The University of Maryland, Baltimore County: http://stories.umbc.edu
- Bucknell University: http://itec.blogs.bucknell.edu/digital-storytelling-in-the-curriculum
- University of Wisconsin, La Crosse: https://www.uwlax.edu/educational-studies/tesol-stories/#tm-221757

Explore digital stories produced by MLs at UMBC: http://stories.umbc.edu/index.php/2009/05/12/esl-stories/

You can also find a number of scholars discuss their research and educational practices using digital stories at meetings of such professional associations as the American Association for Applied Linguistics (AAAL), Teachers of English to Speakers of Other Languages International Association (TESOL International), Washington Area Teachers of English to Speakers of other Languages (WATESOL), New Media Consortium (NMC), and American Communication Association (ACA). All of these examples illustrate the significance of digital storytelling as an educational tool and interesting genre for scholarship.

Digital storytelling process

When getting started with digital storytelling, we need to understand the stages of the process. Lambert and Hessler (2018) describe the steps as:

1. brainstorming ideas for a digital story;
2. exchanging ideas with fellow participants in a story circle;

3. writing a script;
4. collecting visual images;
5. finding music to accompany the verbal and visual narrative elements;
6. storyboarding;
7. recording the audio; and
8. producing a digital story using video editing software.

We have adapted these stages specifically for collaborative work in a language class. In Table 2.1, you will see each phase and step explained with the stages of digital story production. In addition, we include typical activities that can be used in each step and the types of interaction, or collaboration, that typically occur in each step.

Table 2.1 Stages of digital story production in an English language class (Adapted from Vinogradova, 2014)

Phases	*Steps*	*Stage of Digital Story Production*
Pre-planning	Step 1	In class, whole group or small group. Discussions of what digital stories are; watching and analyzing examples; discussing the structure of digital stories; discussion of language(s) used in stories
	Step 2	At home, individual activities. Watching and analyzing examples with worksheets; thinking about themes and content; analyzing language usage
Planning	Step 3	In class, in groups. Story circle – discussion of ideas and possible themes of digital stories; can be multilingual conversations
	Step 4	At home and/or in class, individually. Drafting verbal narratives; thinking and collecting visual images; thinking about possible music; thinking about language(s)
	Step 5	In class, in small groups. Peer review of verbal narratives; can be multilingual conversations
	Step 6	In class and/or at home, individually. Completion of the final draft of verbal narratives; consideration of language(s)
	Step 7	In class and/or at home, individually. Collecting images and visuals for digital stories
	Step 8	In class and/or at home, individually. Storyboarding – creating explicit outlines; combining verbal narrative with images; noting language(s) and subtitles if needed; making notes on possible music
	Step 9	In class, in small groups. Discussion and peer review of storyboards; can be multilingual

(*Continued*)

Table 2.1 (Continued)

Phases	*Steps*	*Stage of Digital Story Production*
Production	Step 10	In class, individually and with peer feedback. Audio recording of verbal narratives; revisiting language choices; getting visual and music components ready
	Step 11	In class, individually and with peer feedback. Digital story production using available tools and materials; adding subtitles as needed
Post-production	Step 12	In class, whole group. Presentations of digital stories and class discussion
	Step 13	Instructor and/or individual and/or peer. Assessment

Lambert (2009) suggests various approaches to undertake and complete these steps. For example, in the brainstorming stage, he suggests using index cards to start writing down ideas to avoid a difficult start of "filling a blank page" (p. 51). Teachers can also set a time limit, for example asking the MLs to draft digital story ideas in ten minutes, or give prompts to create a setting for writing, such as writing a postcard to a friend or a relative about a digital story. Another approach to begin the digital storytelling process is starting with images, such as browsing through photographs or video recordings that can "provoke memories and stories that are meaningful" (Lambert, 2009, p. 53).

The story circle step involves MLs interacting with each other and discussing their ideas for digital stories. This process stimulates MLs to start telling their stories, spontaneously responding to storylines of others and to comments by others about their unshaped narratives and thus prompting them to gradually develop their own storylines. After this stage, MLs move to writing their narratives and selecting their visual images and music.

In storyboarding, MLs visualize their narratives and can see and assess how multiple visual and audio layers of their digital stories come into a multimodal interaction to create a powerful message. This is an important stage in self-assessing and making notes about possible visual and sound effects, additional graphics, and transitions (Lambert, 2009; Lambert & Hessler, 2018). In other words, the storyboard is an explicit outline of a digital story where MLs can see how their multimodal elements come together and convey their intended, powerful meaning.

MLs can choose various ways to produce digital storyboards, including Post-it® notes, photocopies of visual images in combination with excerpts from the voiceover, or a poster board with horizontal lines that represent each layer of a digital story (e.g., images, special effects, transitions, voiceover, etc. [Lambert, 2009]). In our work, we have used PowerPoint software, combining several visual images on a slide with excerpts of the verbal narrative. MLs can also note special effects, transitions, and music on each slide, and then play the slideshow as a digital storyboard to see how all the images work together to support the narrative. These are some effective ways to visualize how multimodal layers of a digital story might interact with each other to create the intended meaning.

The final step in digital story creation is the actual digital production using video editing software. Here teachers can choose to use professional-grade video editing software like Final Cut Pro, software that comes as part of software package on Macintosh or PCs or other freely available software and applications that allow for multimodal composition. At this stage, MLs upload their audio-recorded verbal narratives, musical background, and visual images, combine and sequence them using various video editing techniques, and use visual and audio effects and tools to frame the story and accentuate certain elements. Finally, MLs share their digital stories with each other. In Part II, starting with Chapter 4, we return to each digital storytelling step and cover them in detail with examples, sample materials, and stories from other teachers who have created digital stories with their MLs. We will guide you, language educators, through these stages of digital story production and illustrate how this collaborative and individual work can be incorporated into your language curriculum.

The process of creating a digital story is as important as a digital story itself. It emphasizes the collaborative exchange of ideas, sharing of personal stories and experiences, and creation of a community of practice through the interactive workshop approach (Lambert, 2009; Lambert & Hessler, 2018). In this process, MLs establish an actual dialogue during which every story triggers its own evolution and the development of other stories, creating a continuously evolving multimodal narrative. Working with MLs and following Lambert's (2009) workshop-based collaborative approach, we developed a sequence of the stages of digital story production specifically for language teachers.

In the following featured digital storytelling project, Vanessa Virgiel explains how she used the digital storytelling process to encourage her MLs in South Korea to use English for personal expression. By including the use of avatars, MLs, especially those who might be neurodivergent, feel freer to express themselves and their emotions. Vanessa also explains the software she chose to use and why, and how her MLs translanguaged to develop their stories.

In this chapter, we have explored the history of digital storytelling and briefly looked at the stages of the process of creating a digital story. In the next chapter, we dive more deeply into the theoretical underpinnings of digital storytelling as translanguaging, highlighting the pedagogical power of digital storytelling and how it can be used to support translanguaging. We hope every language teacher can feel confident and prepared to incorporate digital storytelling with translanguaging into language teaching after reading this book.

Featured digital storytelling project: Digital animation project

Name: Vanessa Virgiel
Position: Lecturer, Department of English, Korea Military Academy
Project Location: Seoul, South Korea

When teaching English as a foreign language (EFL) at a military university in Seoul, South Korea, I created the Digital Animation Project with the goal for the cadets to share their stories and use English in a way that was personally meaningful to them. The cadets, high-achieving undergraduate students who undergo frequent military training and live an army lifestyle in preparation for their eventual careers as military officers, seemingly have little extrinsic motivation to use English beyond the need to take the mandatory English classes required for graduation. They share the same mother tongue of Korean, and even most of the international exchange cadets also use Korean as their lingua franca. Moreover, many of them have had negative experiences learning English as a result of the many years of the English for test-taking culture to which South Korean students are subjected. Therefore, I designed the digital animation project as a medium for the cadets to use English collaboratively and creatively. I also wanted it to be a way for those cadets who could be neurodivergent but undiagnosed (due to the extreme social stigma in both Korean and military culture) to be engaged and express themselves in a manner previously unavailable to them. I used the project and adapted it over the course of three semesters, across different courses for freshmen and sophomore cadets.

Each class had approximately 10 to 18 cadets, and I introduced them to the digital animation project through my and later their peers' examples. I chose Plotagon Studio (https://www.plotagon.com) for PC desktop and Plotagon Story for mobile phones as the software for digital storytelling as its design is user friendly and easy to navigate, and it offers features that make creating digital animation *fun*: customizable avatars, various backdrops, character actions (e.g., gestures and facial expressions), sound effects, and the option to either self-record one's own voice or use one of the built-in AI voices. This allowed the cadets to explore different personas or use different avatars to voice their stories, in a manner similar to the way actors can express themselves by inhabiting a character. As such, the cadets could feel a sense of removal as it wasn't *them* telling their story, it was the avatar on the screen. I believe this allowed the cadets to feel freer and be more expressive in a way they couldn't have otherwise. Although the project did not specify a theme or topic that the cadets had to follow, many cadets chose to talk about or parody cadet life in their videos. The cadets utilized translanguaging strategies as they worked together to create their digital animation videos. They switched back and forth between Korean and English as they chose the animation features, negotiated their stories, and considered what they wanted to say and how they wanted to say it. Most of the final videos were in English, though Korean-English wordplay was evident. One group titled their video *Yuktopia*, a portmanteau play on the Korean word *yuksa* (army) and the English word *utopia*, for their video. In end-of-the-semester class watch parties, the cadets (who were the only audience for their creations), had a chance to acknowledge each other's creativity, talent, and voice. They also could recognize those "in" jokes that only other cadets would know.

For others who wish to try undertaking a similar project, I recommend using a software program such as Plotagon, for its affordance as an easy PC desktop app and for the fact that Plotagon Story is also available for both Android (https://play.google.com/store/apps/details?id=com.plotagon.plotagon) and iPhone (https://apps.apple.com/us/app/plotagon-story/id883190178) mobile devices. I would encourage the instructor to play with the software extensively on their own and create their own digital videos that they can share with their students as a means of introducing the software. Perhaps beyond creating loose parameters if it's used as a classroom project, it's wonderful to allow students the challenge and the freedom to create their own stories.

References

Hartley, J., & McWilliam, K. (2009). Computational power meets human contact. In J. Hartley & K. McWilliam (Eds.), *Story circle: Digital storytelling around the world* (pp. 3–15). Wiley-Blackwell.

Lambert, J. (2006). *Digital storytelling: Capturing lives, creating community* (2nd ed.). Digital Diner Press.

Lambert, J. (2009). *Digital storytelling: Capturing lives, creating community* (3rd ed.). Digital Diner Press.

Lambert, J., & Hessler, B. (2018). *Digital storytelling: Capturing lives, creating community* (5th ed.). StoryCenter & Routledge. https://doi.org/10.4324/9781351266369

Nelson, M. E., & Hull, G. (2008). Self-presentation through multimedia: A Bakhtinian perspective on digital storytelling. In K. Lundby (Ed.), *Digital storytelling, mediatized stories: Self-representations in new media* (pp. 123–141). Peter Lang.

Vinogradova, P. (2014). Digital stories in a language classroom: Engaging students through meaningful multimodal projects. *The FLTMAG*. http://fltmag.com/digital-stories

3 Pedagogical Foundations

Translanguaging and Digital Storytelling

In the previous chapter, we outlined the history of digital storytelling as a narrative format often used to share personal, autobiographical stories for community building and social justice. The use of digital storytelling in these ways continues to grow rapidly. In this chapter, we add a focus on digital storytelling as a language classroom project or activity designed to encourage translanguaging. We examine how language education and educators have come to embrace a translanguaging stance and we explore how digital storytelling with translanguaging can improve language learning, develop MLs' critical language awareness, build community in the classroom and beyond, and promote linguistic social justice. With this exploration, we hope to encourage language educators to experience a translanguaging shift in all their classroom actions.

Translanguaging: The Shift to Multilingualism

Over the past 10 to 15 years, the field of language education, especially English language education, has shifted from a monolingual focus to a multilingual focus. Where we used to promote and value only learning the target language, now we recognize the importance of maintaining and strengthening all the languages and varieties of languages that our MLs speak when they come into our classrooms. The theory of translanguaging (García & Li, 2014) has been most influential in making this shift. We now understand the individual benefits of maintaining and strengthening multilingualism, including cognitive benefits, connections among generations of family members, and workforce opportunities (American Academy of Arts & Sciences, 2017). We also recognize the societal benefits of maintaining linguistic diversity and avoiding language loss which "depletes humanity's shared understanding of the world and the varying perspectives and understanding that different languages offer" (Linville & Vinogradova, 2023, p. 226).

While translanguaging is a buzzword in language education, many teachers are still unsure of what it means. Translanguaging is first and foremost a different way of looking at language. Translanguaging values multilingual ways of using languages strategically to make sense of the world,

DOI: 10.4324/9781003295730-4

communicate ideas, and express our individual identity (Li, 2011). As a theory, translanguaging promotes the idea that different languages are not separated in our brains. Rather, we all have a singular, integrated linguistic repertoire that contains all the language elements and features that we know. One way to think about this is to imagine your ability to use English in different situations. Rather than having a compartment for speaking English formally, or in the classroom, or with friends, or for texting, all the English features you know are together. You draw upon them as you need when you communicate, making choices about what and how to communicate depending on the changes in the social situation. To expand this example, all the languages you know are also not in separate compartments in your brain according to the theory of translanguaging. Rather, all your languages are integrated and available for you to use in any communicative situation. You make choices, again, of what to say and how to say it, drawing upon all the elements and features holistically as you navigate your life, minute by minute, day by day. With this view, language learning should not be viewed as adding a language nor should we ignore the other languages MLs know. Instead, language learning should be seen as adding to the number of language features that can be used, and expanding MLs' range of when and where they can use them. The sum of the language features is referred to as the full linguistic repertoire.

Translanguaging as a pedagogy, or an approach to teaching, focuses on expanding MLs' linguistic repertoire to include features of English and developing "linguistic fluidity, dexterity, and identity" (Tian et al., 2020, p. 3). Translanguaging encourages creativity by supporting and encouraging MLs as they explore new, potentially multilingual ways of expressing their thoughts and ideas. Translanguaging also involves criticality, or thinking critically about the ways language has been used and pushing boundaries of what languages can be used in what spaces and how they can be used. Teachers can support MLs as they explore ways to challenge the typical monolingual ways of doing things. For example, MLs can explore using their various languages in assignments that are typically expected to be monolingual in order to convey their deeper understanding and meaning. Li (2011) notes that creativity and criticality "are intrinsically linked: one cannot push or break boundaries without being critical; and the best expression of one's criticality is one's creativity" (p. 1223). Teachers who encourage translanguaging help MLs figure out why and when to push linguistic boundaries to achieve academic learning, the best expression of their identities, and the greatest use of their linguistic repertoire.

Digital Storytelling as Translanguaging

Even with an understanding of translanguaging, teachers may still be unsure of how to incorporate it into their teaching in meaningful ways beyond, "How do you say this in your language?" Digital storytelling is an excellent activity to bring the theory and goals of translanguaging into classrooms, expanding MLs' creativity and criticality as language users. As we saw in Chapter 2, digital storytelling motivates and empowers creators to share their stories and identities, develops multimodal and digital literacy skills, and promotes social justice as it creates connections between creators and their audiences. We further show here how digital storytelling designed with translanguaging improves language learning and academic outcomes, promotes critical language awareness by transcending language boundaries and barriers, and empowers MLs to develop and use their full linguistic repertoire as they claim their place in the community of learners in their classrooms and schools.

> Watch this digital story by an adult migrant to see how translanguaging adds richness and meaning: *Here!*; https://youtu.be/aavW3Tzt58c. Think about how the creator used her two languages and the message that sends about multilingualism. This digital story was produced in Heather and Polina's workshop in summer 2022.

Improving Language Learning and Academic Outcomes

Much has been written about digital storytelling in language classrooms. For example, researchers have explored how digital stories can be rich cultural resources for MLs in content-based English as a second language (ESL) instruction and intercultural communication classes (i.e., Rance-Roney, 2008; Vinogradova et al., 2011). Digital storytelling has also been recognized as useful for language learning and digital literacy development (Anderson et al., 2018; Vinogradova et al., 2011). Digital storytelling with translanguaging can also be used as a teaching resource and a learning project and can lead to improved language learning and academic outcomes for MLs.

As a teaching resource, teachers can show digital stories from the wide variety of online archives referred to in Chapter 2. Teachers can engage in culturally and linguistically responsive teaching (Gay, 2002; Lucas & Villegas, 2013) by choosing digital stories that represent the various languages and cultures in their classroom. MLs can practice language skills as they analyze others' digital stories. They practice listening and reading skills as they watch digital stories in languages their classmates speak and read the subtitles. They practice speaking or writing skills as they analyze the digital stories as narrative texts, for example identifying characters, settings, and major plot points. MLs can also analyze the linguistic choices of digital story creators, in terms of vocabulary, syntax, and discourse, as well as choices of when to use different features or languages from their linguistic repertoire. Most importantly, as MLs view the digital stories they clearly see their teacher's translanguaging stance; that their teacher values other languages and perspectives in the classroom. Representation matters and seeing translanguaging examples from others, how they use their full linguistic repertoire to express meaning, is essential (Seltzer & García, 2020). Teachers can create their own stories as well to show translanguaging at work, blending visual and textual elements to increase learner motivation, understanding, and learning.

As MLs translanguage using their full linguistic repertoire, they are empowered as multilingual individuals to use all their language skills, including English (Rosa & Flores, 2017). In creating their own digital stories, MLs improve their language and academic skills. Each stage of the digital storytelling process is collaborative and can include translanguaging, giving MLs multiple opportunities to interact with others and practice language in meaningful ways. For example, in the story circle, MLs share their story ideas, giving and receiving feedback through oral communication. This is a linguistically complex task and involves a lot of negotiation of meaning as MLs engage in authentic discussions and can translanguage to better communicate their ideas. In later stages of the digital storytelling process, MLs share drafts of their storyboards and multimodal composing, leading to more authentic discussions of meaning and audience, all of which improves their learning outcomes. As a community of practice (Lave & Wenger, 1991), MLs learn from and with each other and come to learn the different strengths (linguistic and/or digital) they each have, developing their confidence at school. Finally, by giving MLs choices about what to communicate and valuing what they say, we create better conditions for language learning (TESOL International Association, 2018).

Promoting Critical Language Awareness

In addition to learning language features, learners need to develop critical language awareness. As Tian et al. (2020) write:

> The goal of English language teaching and learning in the post-multilingualism era is no longer acquiring the native-like form of English and becoming another monolingual, but becoming a competent, multilingual language user who are [sic] aware of and sensitive to the context and could perform fluid, dynamic, and complex language practices with creativity and criticality to achieve their expressive and communicative needs.
>
> (p. 10)

When MLs engage in creating a digital story, they are creative and critical as they choose to use their languages in ways that best express their story. For example, as they craft their narratives, MLs can think about the precise meaning of words in their multilingual repertoire and choose the best word to use, no matter which language it is. Similarly, they can explore combining and new uses of syntax structures across languages, developing a greater awareness of how grammar entails meaning.

When creating a translanguaged digital story, MLs consider how language is a tool of identity. The way we speak indicates who we are and impacts how others see us. We can also choose to use language in particular ways to change how others see us. MLs make choices throughout the digital storytelling process about which language and language features they want to use. In doing so, they develop the ability to sift through the language features available to them and shift their identity as they choose. Similar to how all digital story creators choose which images to include of themselves or to not include any images of themselves in their digital stories, MLs choose how much to reveal of themselves through the language(s) they use. They make critical choices about who their audience is and how they want to communicate as they situate themselves and their stories in the sociocultural environment.

Through the digital storytelling process, MLs can also explore the ways language is a tool of power. MLs will have a sense of how certain languages and language features are more acceptable in society. They will have been told, no doubt, to speak a certain way in school as the assumption is that by doing so they will be more successful. With translanguaged digital storytelling, MLs can challenge this ideology and debate and question which language features they should use in their stories, raising their awareness of the implications of their choices. For example, MLs may want to use *ain't* or other nonstandardized English language forms that are used appropriately in many settings but not often in schools. Teachers who have a translanguaging stance create space for frank discussions of how speakers are perceived when using such forms in different environments and support the development of critical language awareness for MLs and speakers of other varieties of English. As MLs develop a greater understanding of how language usage encodes power and privilege, they learn how to disrupt them by challenging or breaking the rules around language usage. It is important to note that digital storytelling with translanguaging can also be used in classrooms where not every student is an identified ML. Monolingual speakers of English and speakers of varieties of English also need to develop critical awareness of language choices and can do so through translanguaged digital storytelling (Seltzer & García, 2020).

Disrupting Monolingual Ideologies and Empowering MLs

Digital storytelling with translanguaging empowers MLs to use their full linguistic repertoire with pride. Translanguaging through digital storytelling can work "by liberating and privileging language-minoritized speakers' multilingual performances and legitimizing all their linguistic varieties" (Tian et al., 2020, p. 7). We know MLs are often encouraged to use one language over another in educational settings or even punished when they use languages other than English. However, ignoring or demeaning home languages can damage MLs' self-esteem, cognitive development, and is a contributing factor to lower academic achievement (TESOL International Association, 2018). Digital storytelling with translanguaging demonstrates to MLs how valuable their languages are and that they have a place in schools. In addition, digital storytelling can help MLs process complex emotions (Castañeda et al., 2018; Kim & Li, 2021; Vinogradova, 2014), such as experiences of language loss, devaluing of home languages or cultures, and other cultural and linguistic differences they experience. When MLs have the opportunity to tell their story the way they want to tell it, they can "take a step back, from being an actor to being an observer who can make objective decisions about *what* stories should be told [and] *how* they should be told" (Kim & Li, 2021, p. 8). Translanguaged digital stories offer a unique opportunity for MLs to be empowered because of the recognition of their multiple languages.

Digital storytelling with translanguaging can also be a tool for advocacy for MLs, disrupting monolingual ideologies. Translanguaging seeks to dismantle monolingual ideologies that privilege native speakers and to disrupt any hierarchy of languages that prioritizes a particular language or variety of language over another (Tian et al., 2020). We frequently find ways to share our students' stories beyond our classrooms (see Chapter 11 for ideas) and believe this helps others in the school community and beyond to understand MLs' experiences with linguistic and cultural diversity. As such, it is also a tool for peacebuilding in multilingual communities (Vinogradova & Linville, n.d.). Digital storytelling with translanguaging can help change the monolingual mindset and help others see the value of multilingualism.

> Watch *I Belong with Both* (https://www.youtube.com/watch?v=YpjGwtoWfk4) for an exploration of how one multilingual individual manages living in her two countries and languages. This digital story was produced in Heather and Polina's workshop in summer 2022.

When working with MLs to create translanguaged digital stories, it is also important to support them in developing responses when others challenge their language use or choices. For example, teachers can provide opportunities to role play a situation in which they share a translanguaged digital story with someone who reacts negatively to the use of different language features. Someone might comment, "Why isn't this story all in English?" or "I hate reading subtitles." MLs can brainstorm responses such as, "I was really excited to be able to share all of my language knowledge in my story" or "It's important to hear the emotion of my story expressed the way I hear and feel it." Such responses empower MLs and value their language choices while helping others value multilingualism as well.

In the following featured digital storytelling project, Fatima Aldajani explains how she incorporated translanguaging into her digital storytelling project and encouraged the sharing of cultural practices and the building of community among her diverse learners. In addition to having her MLs share their digital stories within the class, she also shared them with the community beyond the classroom with many positive results. As she demonstrates, sharing MLs' multilingual digital stories opens a window toward a future community we imagine where everyone can use their full linguistic repertoire in the ways they are comfortable and empowered to do so. We believe that the use of digital stories as resources and a social networking tool will continue to increase, as digital storytelling is a way to give voice to multilingual individuals everywhere.

We have now covered the theoretical underpinnings of this book and digital storytelling with translanguaging. Including translanguaging in digital storytelling projects is a good way to embrace a translanguaging stance and reap the benefits of translanguaging in language classrooms with MLs. In Part II of the book, we guide you in including translanguaging in each step of the digital storytelling process to improve MLs' language learning, develop their critical language awareness, build community in the classroom and beyond, and promote linguistic social justice. We start in Chapter 4 with preparing you, as a teacher, to incorporate a digital storytelling project with translanguaging in your language classroom.

Featured digital storytelling project: Digital stories with high school refugee and immigrant students

Name: Fatima Aldajani
Position: ESL Adjunct Instructor, American Language Institute, University of Toledo
Project Location: Toledo, Ohio, USA

I teach the course *Oral Communication* to intermediate high-school refugee and immigrant students ages 16–20. The diverse backgrounds of the students create a culturally rich and diverse learning environment. The course covers different topics such as metacognition as a learning habit, cultural aspects, art and identity, social media, and personality. In the course, I asked students to create a short video or audio recording exploring their own sense of identity and how their cultural background, personal experiences, and the course material have shaped it. This digital storytelling project encouraged ESL students to explore connections between their personal experiences, learning, and belonging. It also fostered critical reflection and helped students make meaningful connections between course content and their experiences. Thus, this project aimed to promote student-centered learning and helped students understand their learning needs and experiences. With the use of popular video editing software such as Microsoft MovieMaker and iMovie, students could bring their stories to life.

Students were encouraged to brainstorm ideas and themes they wanted to explore through their stories and collect digital materials such as photos, videos, audio recordings, and written text to help tell the story. I encouraged students to express their perspectives and embrace their creativity through digital storytelling in multiple languages or use a combination of languages within the same story. I also encouraged students to use their first language alongside the target language to express themselves more fully. For example, students could use a mix of English and their first language to talk about the cultural practices and beliefs that have influenced their sense of identity. The project design enhanced student comprehension and increased their awareness of different communication modes while allowing them to express their own voices. Also, I provided resources and support in both languages to help students understand the key concepts and vocabulary related to identities, such as bilingual glossaries, videos, or articles in both languages and opportunities for students to discuss and share their ideas in small groups. It helped to promote multilingualism and fostered translanguaging and a sense of cultural awareness.

By incorporating translanguaging into the digital storytelling project, students could express their ideas and emotions in their first language and share their culture and experiences with others. The emphasis on multilingualism and translanguaging in the project allowed students to explore themes and reveal their narratives in a complex and meaningful way. As one of the students said,

> Throughout this project, I had the opportunity to share my story and connect with my classmates on a deeper level. As a refugee, I have faced many challenges in my life, but this project has given me the platform to express myself and share my experiences with others. I found that the concept of Neuroplasticity really resonated with me. It was empowering to learn about the brain's ability to adapt and change, which gives me hope for my own ability to learn and grow.
>
> (Digital storytelling project participant)

In addition to having students present their digital stories to the class, I shared the stories at various events including school district professional days, university events, and conferences to celebrate the students' efforts and creativity. Every time I ask my audience to reflect on the stories they have seen and put together an action plan on how they will support and meet the needs of their students. The responses expressed welcoming attitudes toward migrants, refugees, and international students. In addition, they raised awareness of their students' needs and experiences. As a result of such a sharing event, one school district conducted a focused group debrief session with their content area teachers who had ESL students in their classes to discuss and reflect on how they could meet their academic, cultural, and linguistic needs. The sessions resulted in a plan for practical steps, the most important of which was to set quarterly one-on-one meetings with students and their teachers to get to know them better and understand their experiences and language positively. This shows that teachers and school administration appreciated hearing about others who have struggled in their community and took active steps to meet their needs.

To others undertaking a similar project, I suggest starting with a clear and concise outline of the project goals and objectives and a well-defined timeline and budget. Additionally, it is vital to involve students in the project planning process, as they will be able to provide valuable feedback and insights into their learning needs, belonging, and life experience. Those interested in finding out more about my project can contact me at my email: fatima.aldajani@utoledo.edu.

References

American Academy of Arts & Sciences: Commission on Language Learning (2017). *America's languages: Investing in language education for the 21st century*. American Academy of Arts & Sciences. ISBN: 0-87724-112-0. Available at https://www.amacad.org/language

Castañeda, M. E., Shen, X., & Claros Berlioz, E. M. (2018). This is my story: Latinx learners create digital stories during a summer literacy camp. *TESOL Journal*, *9*(4), 1–14. https://doi.org/10.1002/tesj.378

García, O., & Li, W. (2014). *Translanguaging: Language, bilingualism, and education*. Palgrave Macmillan. https://doi.org/10.1057/9781137385765

Gay, G. (2002). Preparing for culturally responsive teaching. *Journal of Teacher Education*, *53*(2), 106–116. https://doi.org/10.1177/0022487102053002003

Kim, D., & Li, M. (2021). Digital storytelling: Facilitating learning and identity development. *Computers in Education*, *8*(1), 33–61. https://doi.org/10.1007/s40692-020-00170-9

Lave, J., & Wenger, E. (1991). *Situated learning: Legitimate peripheral participation*. Cambridge University. http://doi.org/10.1017/CBO9780511815355

Li, W. (2011). Moment analysis and translanguaging space: Discursive construction of identities by multilingual Chinese youth in Britain. *Journal of Pragmatics, 43*, 1222–1235. https://doi.org/10.1016/j.pragma.2010.07.035

Linville, H., & Vinogradova, P. (2023). Supporting multilingualism through translanguaging in digital storytelling. In K. Raza, D. Reynolds, & C. Coombe (Eds.), *Handbook of multilingual TESOL in practice* (pp. 225–236). Springer.

Lucas, T., & Villegas, A. M. (2013). Preparing linguistically responsive teachers: Laying the foundation in preservice teacher education. *Theory into Practice, 52*, 98–109. https://doi.org/10.1080/00405841.2013.770327

Rosa, J., & Flores, N. (2017). Do you hear what I hear?: Raciolinguistic ideologies and culturally sustaining pedagogies. In D. Paris & H. S. Alim (Eds), *Culturally sustaining pedagogies: Teaching and learning for justice in a changing world* (pp. 175–190). Teachers College Press.

Seltzer, K., & García, O. (2020). Broadening the view: Taking up a translanguaging pedagogy with all language-minoritized students. In Z. Tian, L. Aghai, P. Sayer, & J. L. Schiessel (Eds.), *Envisioning TESOL through a translanguaging lens* (pp. 23–42). Springer. https://doi.org/10.1007/978-3-030-47031-9_1

TESOL International Association. (2018). *The 6 Principles for exemplary teaching of English learners: Grades K–12*. TESOL Press. https://www.the6principles.org/

Tian, Z., Aghai, L., Sayer, P., & Schiessel, J. L. (2020). Envisioning TESOL through a translanguaging lens in the era of post–multilingualism. In Z. Tian, L. Aghai, P. Sayer, & J. L. Schiessel (Eds.), *Envisioning TESOL through a translanguaging lens* (pp. 1–20). Springer. https://doi.org/10.1007/978-3-030-47031-9_1

Vinogradova, P. (2014). Digital stories in a language classroom: Engaging students through a meaningful multimodal task. *The FLTMAG*. https://fltmag.com/digital-stories

Vinogradova, P., & Linville, H. A. (n.d.). Digital storytelling for peacebuilding in a multilingual community. *TESOL Journal*. Under review.

Vinogradova, P., Linville, H. L., & Bickel, B. (2011). "Listen to my story and you will know me": Digital stories as student-centered collaborative projects. *TESOL Journal, 2*(2), 173–202. https://doi.org/10.5054/tj.2011.250380

Part II Creating a Digital Story

4 Getting Ready to Go

Teacher Planning and Preparation

Up to this point, we have discussed what digital stories are, the benefits of digital storytelling, and how it can be incorporated into English language instruction. Probably at this point you have decided that you would like to use digital stories in your teaching and incorporate them into your course curriculum. How exciting! But of course, you might be wondering where to start, asking yourself, What do I do first? How shall I prepare for this project? How can I include digital storytelling in my curriculum with realistic expectations? How can I include translanguaging and meet my MLs' language learning needs? In this chapter we address these questions and guide you as you plan for a digital storytelling project in your class. As you start planning, think about the following questions:

- What are the MLs' learning needs and how will a digital storytelling project address them?
- What technology is available to you and MLs in class and outside of class?
- What technology are MLs familiar with and which do they use on a regular basis?
- What are MLs' levels of technological literacy?
- What is your own level of technological literacy? What do you need to learn before asking your MLs to engage with a digital storytelling project?
- What learning objectives will the digital storytelling project enable MLs to meet? How will they meet these learning objectives?
- What language skills will MLs need to successfully complete the digital storytelling process?
- How comfortable are MLs with translanguaging? How can the digital storytelling project encourage MLs to use their full linguistic repertoires?
- What limitations do you have in preparing and implementing a digital storytelling project with your MLs?
- How will you scaffold the digital storytelling project throughout the class?
- What do you need to do to prepare for the digital storytelling work with your MLs?

DOI: 10.4324/9781003295730-6

MLs' Learning Needs in Digital Storytelling Projects

Mapping MLs' learning needs and connecting them with digital storytelling projects is an important starting point, but might also be quite puzzling, especially if you have never used multimodal projects in your classes. Perhaps a good place to start is your course learning objectives. Depending on where you teach, these learning objectives might be provided to you, or you might have to develop your own as you prepare to teach your class. Regardless, thinking about learning objectives is a good starting point, and probably one that is familiar to you.

So let's first answer the question: What do I want my MLs to be able to do with (1) language; (2) content; and/or (3) skills by the end of this class? List and organize these learning objectives in a form that is useful and convenient to you. You may use the sentence starter, "MLs will be able to … " for each one. After you have clarified the learning objectives for your class, the next step is to outline learning objectives specifically for the digital storytelling project. What do you want the MLs to accomplish through this project? What will your MLs be able to do as a result of creating their own digital stories? An option is first to think about the digital storytelling format and steps the students will have to go through in developing them and think what the learning outcomes of that work would be. You may want to refer back to Table 2.1 in Chapter 2. Based on these steps, we suggest the following digital storytelling learning objectives.

By the end of the digital storytelling project, MLs will be able to:

1. Brainstorm thoughts and ideas relevant to the topic they are working on,
2. Outline thoughts and ideas relevant to the topic they are working on,
3. Talk and write about important aspects of their lives,
4. Offer suggestions and peer feedback and respond to suggestions in a constructive way (if doing peer reviews),
5. Compose a multimodal personal narrative,
6. Select and use necessary technology tools to compile relevant multimodal components,
7. Store and organize multimodal information for easy access and navigation, and
8. Use video editing software to produce a multimodal narrative.

Please note that these are only suggestions; your MLs' language levels and technological abilities will determine your exact digital storytelling objectives. For example, if you are working with MLs at beginning levels of English language proficiency, you might need to modify the expectations with respect to peer review. These are found in learning objective number 4 in the list above and the peer review step in Table 2.1. Your MLs might not have the necessary level of English language proficiency to engage in peer review without scaffolding. Language level is certainly an important consideration in determining your digital storytelling objectives. However, rather than removing the learning objective, we encourage you to modify it, doing peer reviews even if your MLs are beginner learners. Ways to do this include having MLs use their home languages for peer review, a great opportunity for translanguaging, or scaffolding the peer review, for example, by using a worksheet, Padlet, or Jamboard activity, and introducing MLs to some relevant and useful expressions in English. Peer review, even modified, allows MLs to practice the useful skills of giving and responding to suggestions.

Now that you have listed your course and your digital storytelling project learning objectives, you can compare the two lists. It could be useful to organize them in a table to see the overlaps and gaps, and to identify the MLs' needs informed by the learning objectives. This becomes the first step in the mapping of a digital storytelling project in your class. In Table 4.1, we provide an example of how learning objectives and MLs' learning needs can be outlined and aligned. In this example, we use WIDA standards (WIDA, 2020; https://wida.wisc.edu/teach/standards/eld) to identify the course learning objective, which would be relevant for K-12 setting for many US states. If you are teaching in a different setting, you are likely to be using a different source for your learning objectives (e.g., learning outcomes for your level and the course).

Some of you might need to get administrative permission to do a digital storytelling project. In addition, you may need to show how digital storytelling can tie into your curriculum. We believe there are strong connections to most subject areas. In Table 4.2 we provide some examples of how to connect digital storytelling to content standards in a variety of subject areas.

Table 4.1 Mapping learning objectives and MLs' needs

Course learning objectives	*Digital Storytelling (DS) project learning objectives*	*MLs' learning needs (language, technology, content)*	*Planning notes*
Example: WIDA ELD Standard 2: Language for Language Arts (ELD-LA.4-5. Inform. Expressive) MLs construct informative texts that introduce and define a topic for a specific audience. (WIDA, 2020, p. 114)	Example: Brainstorm thoughts and ideas relevant to the topic of MLs' DS	Example: - Be able to identify topics and themes of personal significance - Be able to identify keywords and key concepts for their stories - Be able to write brainstorming notes - Be able to use word processing software and type their notes	*Add notes here specific to your teaching context.*

Table 4.2 Sample content standard connections for digital storytelling projects

Subject area	*Content standard*	*Digital storytelling connection*
Social studies	Theme 1: Culture Theme 4: Individual development and identity Theme 9: Global Connections (National Council for the Social Studies, 2020)	–Middle school MLs can watch several digital stories created by individuals from a particular place/cultural group and draw conclusions about cultural impacts on storytelling and identity development.
English language arts	Standards for Writing • Writing for a particular audience • Producing clear and coherent writing Standards for Speaking and Listening • Communicating appropriate to task, purpose, and situation • Explaining language choices Standards for Language • Understanding how language functions differently depending on context • Explaining language choices (National Governors Association Center for Best Practices, Council of Chief State School Officers, 2010a)	–5th grade MLs can write their digital storytelling narrative for a particular audience and edit their work (optionally with a peer) to ensure the narrative is clear and coherent. –8th grade MLs can think about how their narrative recording for their digital story engages their audience, and re-record as necessary. MLs can also discuss and explain their language choices, especially those related to translanguaging. –12th grade MLs can analyze the context of their digital story, thinking about audience, genre, and purpose, and explain language choices with respect to vocabulary, grammar, and translanguaging.
Math	Domain: Measurement and data Standard: Represent and interpret data (National Governors Association Center for Best Practices, Council of Chief State School Officers, 2010b)	–3rd grade MLs can record the length of time (seconds and minutes) images are on the screen or the length of time of transitions between images in a table. MLs can compare data across various digital stories.
Art	Anchor Standard 8: Interpret intent and meaning in artistic work. Anchor Standard 11: Relate artistic ideas and works with societal, cultural and historical context to deepen understanding. (National Coalition for Core Arts Standards, 2023)	–Secondary-level MLs can watch each other's digital stories and discuss the meaning behind each story. After understanding each other's digital stories, MLs can relate the ideas shared in the stories to their current context as MLs.

Technology Availability and Needs

The second step in this digital storytelling project preparation work is assessing MLs' technology needs for the project and the technology available. Keep in mind the technology needs that are specific to digital storytelling projects, as dictated by the digital story format: an audio recorded verbal narrative, visuals of any format, music background, and various visual and audio special effects combined into a multimodal narrative using video editing software.

Technology Needed for Digital Story Projects

1. Desktops/laptops/tablets
2. Software for word processing (e.g., Word, Google Docs) and creation of slide presentations (e.g., PowerPoint, Google Slides)
3. Audio recording equipment (e.g., a voice recording app on a smartphone, a digital Dictaphone, Audacity on a desktop or laptop)
4. Photography and video recording equipment (if students want to take and use their own pictures and videos). Smartphones usually work well for this.
5. Ways to save and organize files. If using tablets or Chromebooks, we recommend organizing all work on Google Drive.
6. Video editing software. This requires the most consideration and depends on the hardware you are using for your projects. Some commonly used video editing applications for digital storytelling work are iMovie and Final Cut Pro (if using a Mac computer or iPad), WeVideo (a web-based video editing application with free and paid versions), and PowerDirector (a web-based video editing application with free and paid versions). To make your decision on video editing software, you will need to explore each application to evaluate ease and complexity of navigation, availability of tools, and costs. Free versions of some web-based applications might be quite limiting in the number of tools they offer, while others might offer just the necessary tools and intuitive ways of video editing suitable for any type of learner including the ones with limited technology skills. (See more on choosing your video editing software in Chapter 8.)

Google Drive (https://www.google.com/drive/) has several advantages for digital storytelling work.

1. Easily accessible using Gmail account which many MLs will already have;
2. Files are accessible anywhere on any device as long as there is internet connection;

3. Very high storage capacity for images and music;
4. Easy to use and has built-in interface with some video editing tools such as PowerDirector;
5. MLs often already know the tool and associated software;
6. Learning this tool will help in other situations where Google Drive is used; and
7. Some institutions already use it as part of Google Classroom.

As you are evaluating available technology, be sure to determine whether you will need permission to use any of the technology available and whether someone will need or be available, to help you with the technology during the project. In addition, you need to identify if the technology is available to all your MLs in your educational setting. This also includes finding out what technology is available to MLs outside of school. It is important to note here that digital storytelling projects, while being highly collaborative, are individual projects and require MLs to have individual access to technology and video editing software. Here are some questions you might find useful to answer while assessing technology availability and needs in your context:

- How many MLs do you have in your class? How do you plan on grouping the MLs, if necessary?
- What hardware and software do MLs have access to at school, at home, and in a community setting (e.g., community library, community center)? How easy is this access?
- What technology do MLs use on a regular basis for educational, communication, and entertainment purposes?
- What are the MLs' levels of technological literacy?
- What technology are you comfortable and not comfortable using?

We provide here the chart we use (Table 4.3) to help you build a comprehensive technology picture in preparation for your digital storytelling project.

If you are working in a teaching context where technology availability is quite limited or class sizes are quite large, you might consider splitting your class into smaller groups to work on the digital storytelling project. For example, one day MLs in Group A work on revising and peer-reviewing their verbal narratives or audio recording their narratives while MLs in Group B are working on computers to finalize their digital story maps and organize visuals they plan on using in their digital stories. In this way, MLs can still enjoy the benefits of digital storytelling even in resource-constrained environments.

Table 4.3 Technology teaching context chart

	In the school	*In your classroom*	*To your students*	*Other*
Equipment:				
What technology is available immediately?				
What technology is available daily?				
What technology is available weekly or less frequently?				
Software:				
What software is available for use?				
What software needs to be acquired/ installed?				
What access is there to online applications and programs?				
What permission/ funding must be gained to install software?				
Access and Permissions:				
What permission must be gained to use equipment/software?				
What training is necessary to use equipment/software?				
What accounts need to be set up for students and teachers for the project?				
Other Considerations:				
How many MLs will you have in your class?				
How do you plan on grouping the MLs, if necessary?				
What cultural expectations are there with technology?				
What allies can you identify to help you work with technology?				

Technological Literacy

The next step in the preparation process is to understand the levels of technological literacy that MLs have. This helps in planning, setting up realistic expectations about the project, and identifying the types of technological support you will need to offer MLs during the project.

> **A note on technological and digital literacies**
>
> Traditionally, literacy is viewed as an ability to read and write. But as Jones and Hafner (2012) emphasize, literacy, or rather literacies, go beyond that and mean creating different types of meanings, establishing different kinds of relationships, and enacting "different types of social identities" (p. 12). While technological literacy refers to the ability to use various digital tools successfully, to achieve a particular task, digital literacies "involve … the ability to adapt the affordances and constraints to digital tools to particular circumstances" (p. 13). This adaptation requires creativity and critical understanding of digital tools and environments in which they are used. To set up a successful digital storytelling project, teachers need to know MLs' levels of technological literacy—what digital tools they are able to use and what they can create using these digital tools. Development of digital literacies can be one of the goals of digital storytelling and it can be carefully scaffolded within the project.

If you have MLs with rather high levels of technological literacy, and if they have access to necessary technology outside of class, you might not need to spend time in class on steps of digital story production that involve work with technology. The MLs will be able to manage the digital storytelling steps and work with video editing software on their own following brief in-class demonstrations and provided guidelines. These are the MLs who regularly use computers and tablets to complete various academic tasks, run online searches, manage blogs or vlogs, use social media, do digital photography, and overall use technology on a day-to-day basis. In contrast, you might have MLs with low technological literacy skills. For these MLs, digital storytelling projects become not only wonderful opportunities for self-expression and language development, but also important opportunities for the development of technological literacy skills. These are the MLs who might not be using computers and tablets on a regular basis and might not have computers in their homes. They might have smartphones and might be able to make phone calls; text; send and receive emails; take, send, and receive pictures; and use various smartphone applications (e.g., WhatsApp and Telegram). They might also be using social media applications like Facebook and Instagram. However, typing up a

Word document, developing a PowerPoint presentation, manipulating a mouse, saving and organizing files, and other skills might be new and unfamiliar to them.

There are various ways to find out the technological literacy skills of your MLs, such as observations, surveys, or interviews. If you had the same MLs in previous classes, you might already have an idea of what's possible and what's new to them through in-class observations and conversations. Regardless of how well we think we know our MLs and their familiarity with technology, it is useful to collect information using a survey. Here are some sample questions you can include in your survey. You can also make your survey multilingual to ensure the accuracy of collected information as well as to welcome students' home language into the classroom and the digital storytelling process from the very beginning.

Sample survey questions:

1. What technology do you use on a daily basis? (desktop computer, laptop computer, tablet, iPad, Chromebook, smartphone, digital camera, digital voice recorder, other)
2. What technology do you have at home?
3. What technology do you use at work?
4. What technology do you use to complete your schoolwork?
5. What technology are you most comfortable using?
6. What technology can you teach someone to use?
7. What activities do you do with technology on a daily basis? (Send and receive emails; make phone calls; write notes; use a calendar; use public transportation applications; use navigation and mapping applications; take pictures; record audio (e.g., voice notes, your thoughts); record videos; edit video recordings; post on social media; write papers; develop presentations; complete schoolwork; write a journal; write a blog; play games; talk to family and friends on WhatsApp, Skype, Zoom, Telegram; other)
8. What is your most favorite thing to do using technology?
9. What is your least favorite thing to do using technology?
10. What do you worry about when using technology?
11. What help do you need when using technology?

Making Your Own Digital Story

Another important step in preparing for the digital storytelling project in your class is making your own digital story. It is great if you have already made one. But if you have not, or if you are doing a digital storytelling project in a new teaching context, it is particularly important that you make your own digital story. First of all, you will experience the joys and challenges of the process that your MLs will experience in your class. It is a useful and humbling experience to put ourselves into our MLs' shoes.

Second, you will gain a better understanding of the nuances of the process, of how video editing software works, and what challenges you and your MLs might face in the particular context. Third, you will have a digital story to show your MLs as a model. In our experience, MLs enthusiastically respond to digital stories produced by their instructors. They are excited to learn new and personal information about us and to see our own vulnerability. Using our own stories also becomes an excellent way to model the digital storytelling process and activities. For example, Polina developed a new digital story, *What is Home?* (https://www.youtube.com/watch?v=T8EMZTdW8XI), and shared it in our digital storytelling workshop for the "We Live in La Crosse: Stories of Belonging" project. One of the activities we used in the digital storytelling workshop was asking our MLs to describe their homes using a five senses poem format, answering the following questions:

- What does your home look like?
- What does your home smell like?
- What does your home feel like?
- What does your home sound like?
- What does your home taste like?

Polina demonstrated how the five sentences could be integrated into a digital multimodal narrative through her own digital story. In addition to having a model for the MLs, creating a new digital story also allowed Polina to explore the PowerDirector software in more detail and understand how it works and what free features it has when used on an Apple computer. Before this, she had used PowerDirector as an application on iPad and Chromebook, which has slightly different features and possibilities as compared to the full computer version. This software exploration also allowed her to prepare and record two instructional videos for the MLs on how to edit audio components in the PowerDirector project timeline (See Figure 4.1 for an example). For this video, she used some stock images and music available in PowerDirector and the voiceover from her own digital story.

Before beginning to work with MLs, be sure you know how to do the following in your chosen application:

- Import images/video/music;
- Set images into the timeline and move them around;
- Increase or decrease the length of time each image/video is on the screen;
- Choose and change transitions between images/videos;
- Set the voiceover into the timeline;
- Set the music into the timeline;
- Insert breaks into the voiceover and music if needed;
- Increase or decrease volume of the voiceover and music;

Figure 4.1 Screenshot of an instructional video. Image by Polina Vinogradova.

- Add subtitles;
- Create a title slide;
- Add credits;
- Save the project; and
- Share (export) the project.

Based on your experience and your knowledge of the MLs, you can develop a digital storytelling manual or a series of short instructional videos for the MLs to follow in their digital storytelling process. Developing your own digital story and producing it using the same video editing software as you plan on using with your MLs allows you to test the digital storytelling process and better understand what steps of the digital storytelling project MLs can engage in independently and where they will need extra guidance and assistance from you.

Mapping a digital story project

By now, you have done substantial preparations for a digital storytelling project in your class. The last step in this robust preparation process is mapping how you will integrate the digital storytelling project into your course curriculum. Following is an example of a chart that you can use for project mapping (Table 4.4). We have outlined the first two steps as an example of how project mapping can be done and how activities and digital storytelling can be incorporated in planning. Feel free to modify and adjust this table depending on the length of your course, your course content, the focus of your digital storytelling project, and your MLs' needs.

Table 4.4 Digital storytelling project mapping chart example for intercultural communication class for university-level international MLs

Weeks	*Course content & activities*	*Digital storytelling (DS) step*	*DS activities*	*DS examples to show*
1	Introduction to course Course expectations Definitions of culture	Step 1: Introduction to DS	- Icebreaker: Multimodal & multilingual table tents about you - Watching sample DS - Brainstorming: What element of culture might you explore in your digital story?	DS explanation video (https://www.youtube.com/watch?v=e5usc00wa40) Instructor's DS
2	Exploring US academic culture	Step 2: DS analysis Thinking further about topics and themes of students' DS	- Watching sample DS - Completing worksheets (Figures 5.1 and 5.2) - Brainstorming (possible pair work): Emotional response to DS - Further thinking about your DS	*Home* by Heather Linville: https://youtu.be/2eAT4X-Na84 *My Story of Jing Di Zhi Wa* by Xinyu (Amber) Wang: https://www.youtube.com/watch?v=ILds0KnCTRI&list=PLpLYwGjO8th66-4r9-ab-BzHlKlhXbnA2&t=1s

Here, we suggest that you look back at Table 2.1 in Chapter 2 as it outlines the steps of digital story production. These steps should guide you in developing your project mapping chart.

Mapping your digital storytelling project

Using the template in Table 4.4, do preliminary mapping of your digital storytelling project. Use Table 2.1 to outline the digital storytelling steps and, if you already know your course content and schedule, start outlining the course content week by week. As you do this work, consider the following: What do you need to know to complete the mapping? What resources or help do you need to complete it? We suggest you save the template and keep working on it gradually as you continue reading this book. As you go through the chapters and examples, you will be able to further populate your course map with ideas for activities and DS resources.

In the project mapping table, it is very useful to list your course content by week and then list digital storytelling steps from Table 2.1. This will allow you to see how digital storytelling steps can be integrated and will correlate with the course content. As you map the course, you will discover if it makes more sense to introduce the digital storytelling project to MLs on day one or to wait for a week or several classes to bring in the project and start working on it. Whatever you choose to do, a course map like this will allow you to outline the steps, identify materials you will need, develop necessary activities, and make changes to your plan depending on how the course progresses. Having a course map like this also allows us to think more about what other resources, help, and support we might need in this process.

In the following featured digital storytelling project, Dana Saito-Stehberger and Clare Jimeno explain how they incorporate digital storytelling into the *Elementary Computing for All* curriculum for their 4th and 5th grade classes. By combining digital storytelling and the goals of the computing curriculum, MLs were motivated to learn computer coding skills and develop their language skills, and also benefited from learning about each other.

In this chapter, we have focused on preparing you, the teacher, for the digital storytelling project you want to implement in your class. We hope you can envision a successful digital storytelling project in your classroom! In the next chapter, we focus on preparing MLs for digital storytelling. We help you consider the technological and language skills, motivation, and knowledge they will need to make your digital storytelling project a success.

Featured digital storytelling project: Elementary computing for all

Name: Dana Saito-Stehberger and Clare Jimeno
Position: Director of Curriculum and Professional Development at the Digital Learning Lab at the University of California, Irvine (Dana) and 5th grade GATE teacher at Muir Fundamental Elementary School in Santa Ana Unified School District (Clare)
Project Location: Irvine, California, USA

This project was funded by the National Science Foundation (#1738825z) and the United States Department of Education (#U411C190092).

In a school district in southern California where 45% of the students are designated multilingual learners (MLs) and 87% come from low-income families, the Elementary Computing for All (ECforALL) curriculum is taught to 4th and 5th graders to introduce computer coding. The ECforALL curriculum guides students to build original projects in block-based Scratch coding language. We strategically integrated storytelling with the computing curriculum as it has been shown in classroom settings to increase motivation, empathy, and confidence (Hung et al., 2012; Sadik, 2008; Sukovic, 2014), particularly with elementary-aged students.

One of the projects in the ECforALL curriculum is the About Me project. It encourages students to animate the characters and talk about their interests and hobbies using recorded audio or text using Scratch (https://scratch.mit.edu/). Students are motivated to build their projects when they see the example projects with backgrounds, characters, movement, and sound that can be manipulated. Students are encouraged to communicate in the language of their choice or a mixture of languages. Often, projects reflect students' cultural identities by sharing aspects they value through their narrated experiences, interests, and expressions of consciousness about their skills (Ojeda Ramirez et al., 2023). View an example About Me project at bit.ly/aboutmeExample.

Another Scratch project that incorporates the storytelling process is the Change Maker project. After studying examples of change makers in history, students chose and researched their own change maker to report on through a Scratch project. As a class, students decided on essential questions to address, and they created storyboards as they planned their projects. Some topics included Cesar Chavez, Yuri Kochikama, and Medgar Evers. View an example Change Maker project at: bit.ly/medgarevers

Scratch is a collaborative environment and as soon as the coder clicks the orange "share" button, it is accessible to the public. Scratch projects are easily shared with others by copying and pasting the URL into a text or email. Students can share their projects with each other in their classrooms in a gallery walk and exchange of feedback. Classmates enjoy learning details about one another and discussing how certain codes were created.

Although embracing digital storytelling projects has its challenges, such as the time it takes to understand the technology and for students to develop their creative ideas, the benefits for MLs far outweigh them. Some MLs who were reluctant readers and writers in the classroom became avid Scratchers. They were eager to tell their stories through the medium of recorded voice, text bubbles, and animated characters. To those students, the Scratch environment changed ordinary tasks such as writing and presenting a report into a project they were excited to work on. Another benefit is the students' interest in each other's projects. It is always uplifting to be recognized like this by classmates. In addition, MLs' speaking and pronunciation skills benefit greatly from this project as students record and re-record their narratives until they are satisfied.

If you are interested in teaching your students Scratch so they can create the storytelling projects described above, go to bit.ly/scratchBasics for free access to lesson plans, slide decks, and student workbooks. For more information on how this curriculum was developed specifically for multilingual learners, see Saito-Stehberger et al. (2021).

References

Hung, C. M., Hwang, G. J., & Huang, I. (2012). A project-based digital storytelling approach for improving students' learning motivation, problem-solving competence and learning achievement. *Educational Technology & Society*, *15*(4), 368–379.

Ojeda Ramirez, S., Tsan, J., Eatinger, D., Jacob, S., Saito-Stehberger, D., & Franklin, D. (2023). Describing elementary students' spheres of influence in Scratch "About me" projects. In *2023 Proceedings of the ACM SIGCSE Technical Symposium on Computer Science Education*. https://doi.org/10.1145/3545945.3569869

Sadik, A. (2008). Digital storytelling: A meaningful technology-integrated approach for engaged student learning. *Educational Technology Research and Development*, *56*(4), 487–506. doi:10.1007/s11423-008-9091-8

Saito-Stehberger, D., Garcia, L., & Warschauer, M. (2021). Modifying curriculum for novice computational thinking elementary teachers and English language learners. In *Proceedings of the 26th ACM Conference on Innovation and Technology in Computer Science Education* (Vol. 1, pp. 136–142).

Sukovic, S. (2014). iTell: Transliteracy and digital storytelling. *Australian Academic and Research Libraries*, *45*(3), 205–229.

References

Jones, R. H., & Hafner, C. A. (2012). *Understanding digital literacies: A practical introduction*. Routledge. https://doi.org/10.4324/9780203095317

National Coalition for Core Arts Standards (2023). *National core arts standards: A conceptual framework for arts learning*. https://www.nationalartsstandards.org/

National Council for the Social Studies (2020). *National curriculum standards for social studies: A framework for teaching, learning, and assessment*. NCSS Publications.https://www.socialstudies.org/standards/national-curriculum-standards-social-studies

National Governors Association Center for Best Practices, Council of Chief State School Officers (2010a). *Common core state standards for English language arts*. http://corestandards.org/

National Governors Association Center for Best Practices, Council of Chief State School Officers (2010b). *Common core state standards for mathematics*. http://corestandards.org/

WIDA (2020). *WIDA English language development standards framework, 2020 edition, Kindergarten-grade 12*. Board of Regents of the University of Wisconsin System. https://wida.wisc.edu/teach/standards/eld

5 Preparing Learners for the Task

Now that you have considered the elements important for preparing yourself, as a teacher, to implement a digital storytelling project in your classroom, the next step is to prepare your learners. We suggest you consider five areas in your preparation: ML motivation, knowledge of digital storytelling, language skills for digital storytelling (e.g., composing a personal narrative, giving feedback, brainstorming, etc.), technological skills for digital storytelling, and permissions. In addition to the technological considerations we outlined in Chapter 4, consider the following questions to aid in your planning:

- How will I generate excitement for the digital storytelling project?
- How will I motivate and engage my MLs to do their best?
- What knowledge do my MLs already have about digital storytelling?
- Have any of my MLs created a digital story, or another type of digital product, already?
- What are my MLs' language level(s) in each of their languages?
- In what ways will MLs need to be able to use language to successfully complete the digital storytelling process?
- What languages and language features do my MLs have at their disposal?
- What digital storytelling skills will my MLs need to be able to successfully complete their digital story?
- What permissions will my MLs need to use images and videos in their digital stories?
- What permissions will I need to share my MLs' digital stories in the school and community?

Motivation and Engagement

The most important consideration in preparing learners for a digital storytelling project is their motivation and excitement for the task. Dörnyei (2018) points out that the distractions of the 21st century have "bombarded [young people] with information through multiple channels and the pace of social life has been intensified by the social media in an unprecedented

DOI: 10.4324/9781003295730-7

manner." It is therefore essential that teachers motivate MLs to get them interested in learning, and then engage MLs to ensure they stay focused on the learning task, "cutting through the multitude of distractions." Dörnyei (2018) points out that creating a feeling of ownership, personalizing teaching materials, raising curiosity and interest, applying project-based learning, using technology, and creating opportunities for MLs to engage with each other in meaningful ways are important for ML engagement. We have related these ideas to five ways digital storytelling inspires most MLs, gets them excited for a digital storytelling project, and keeps them engaged:

1. Digital storytelling is a creative task in which MLs get to choose or create images and music and use technology creatively (capturing the benefits of project-based learning, raising curiosity and interest, and using technology);
2. Digital storytelling is a task full of choices in which MLs have final say and control over each aspect of the final product (what Dörnyei might refer to as a feeling of ownership);
3. Digital storytelling is a personally meaningful task in which MLs get to share their own ideas and stories (the most personalized of all teaching materials—those created by MLs themselves!);
4. Digital storytelling is a task in which collaboration is built into each stage and is needed (creating opportunities for meaningful interaction among MLs); and
5. Digital storytelling is a task in which success can be guaranteed (and a high grade) if MLs just complete it.

Knowing your MLs, you will determine which aspect or aspects of the project will be most motivating and engaging to them. You can choose a few or use them all! In any case, we suggest beginning to "talk up" the project at least three weeks to a month before you begin. Here are some ideas of how to do so, based on what you think will engage your MLs best.

If you think your MLs will be motivated by:

- *Creativity*
  Tell MLs that in the next project they will have the chance to listen to a lot of music and choose songs to match the mood of a story. Have them read a story and choose a piece of music to go with it, as a preparatory activity. Show a digital story that has many different elements. For example, the digital story *Who Am I as an English Language Teacher* utilizes a variety of creative multimodal techniques: https://vimeo.com/444992145. This digital story was produced in Polina's class in summer 2020.
- *Choice*
  Tell MLs that in the next project, they are in charge of selecting or creating all the elements that will be included, and that they have the

final say. As an example, choose a topic to discuss in class and then ask MLs to go on the Internet and find an image that they think would help someone understand the topic. Accept all images as good aids for understanding and highlight how each ML's image may be different but just as valid. Show a digital story that you might have done differently (e.g., might have used different images, music, or other elements). For example, the digital story *Remaking El Rancho* does not use music and relies on visuals and verbal narrative in its meaning development: https://www.youtube.com/watch?v=5IrKOS5jJao.

- *Personal storytelling*
  Tell MLs that they will be learning much about each other in the next project as each person gets to tell their own story. Ask them to each bring in a picture, printed out or on a device, to the next class period and spend some time sharing with each other the story behind the image they brought. Show your own story, if you already have one, or another in which a lot can be learned in just two to three minutes. For example, the digital story *Learning a New Language to Change My Future* is personal and powerful: https://www.youtube.com/watch?v=mFS2PhUGG2k&t=2s. This digital story was produced in Debora Amidani's class in summer 2022 (see Featured Digital Storytelling Project at the end of this chapter).
- *Collaboration*
  Explain how the classroom will become a community of practice (see more in Chapter 9) in which each ML brings their unique strengths and weaknesses and everyone learns from each other. Find a technological skill that you are weak in, and then find out in the classroom which MLs can help you learn it, highlighting how even you are a part of the community of practice in the classroom and will be learning alongside them. Show a story where family or friend collaboration was essential. The digital story *Living the Dream* is an excellent example of the creator's collaboration with her husband, who drew all the images for her digital story: https://vimeo.com/265269480. This digital story was produced in Polina's class in spring 2016.
- *Success*
  Tell your MLs that there is no right or wrong way to create a digital story, that they are expected to learn from and with each other (and it's not seen as cheating), and that each of them will be successful just by completing the project (see Chapter 11 for more on assessment and evaluation of digital stories). You may want to talk individually with each ML about their current grade and how it will go up after completing their digital story. Show a digital story and discuss how difficult it is to give a grade and how it would get full marks because it is complete, but not perfect. The digital story *How I Become an ArmyBlink Girl in My Life* is an example you might want to use: https://youtu.be/ppXrTlsDqGg. This digital story was produced in Heather and Polina's workshop in summer 2022.

As a final note on motivation and engagement, we believe it is important for teachers to create digital stories alongside MLs or use previously created examples for them to view. We discuss the rationale for this in detail in Chapter 4. Digital storytelling is personal work and sharing stories makes us vulnerable. Teachers must be willing to put themselves in a vulnerable position, engage in this work, and share their own stories if they ask their MLs to do so.

> Find our digital stories here: Polina's https://youtu.be/T8EMZTdW8XI, Heather's https://youtu.be/2eAT4X-Na84.

Knowledge for Digital Storytelling

The first step to prepare MLs to create their own digital story is to have them watch and analyze other stories. This is essential if you are working with MLs who have never created a digital story before. We suggest first identifying two stories that you think will be interesting to your MLs, and then creating worksheets like the following examples to have MLs analyze the elements, learning what is involved in digital storytelling and conceptualizing how they will make their own. You can choose digital stories from rich online collections listed in Chapter 2.

Sample worksheet for digital story (DS) analysis

DS Worksheet 1: Home

Digital Story by Heather Linville: https://youtu.be/2eAT4X-Na84
Directions: Watch Dr. Heather's digital story and answer the questions.

1. What <u>elements</u> are in the digital story? (Circle all the elements you see and hear).
   a. Personal photos
   b. Images from the Internet
   c. Video clips
   d. Music
   e. Cartoons
   f. Gifs
   g. Written words
   h. Dr. Heather's voice
2. Who is the story about? (Circle one).
   a. Dr. Heather's dad
   b. Dr. Heather

   c. Dr. Heather's husband
   d. People in Mexico, Spain, and Panama
3. What is the main topic of this digital story? (Circle one).
   a. Dr. Heather's experience learning languages
   b. Dr. Heather's feeling of home
   c. Dr. Heather's experience as a teacher
   d. Dr. Heather's experience living in different countries
4. How long was this story excluding the credits? How about including the credits?
5. What languages were used in Dr. Heather's story?
6. What emotions did you experience when watching Dr. Heather's digital story?
7. Why do you think Dr. Heather made this digital story? What was the purpose of it?
8. What else did you notice about Dr. Heather's digital story?

After watching and analyzing the first digital story, MLs have a sense of what elements can be included, what topics could be shared, how digital stories evoke emotional responses, and the purpose of telling a digital story. To challenge more experienced storytellers, you may have them analyze the different types of transitions between images in the story, and why different types could be used. You can additionally ask MLs to pinpoint what element(s) caused the emotion(s) they felt. With each question, MLs are learning more about what is possible in their own digital stories.

For the second analysis, we suggest choosing a digital story that is quite different from the first in terms of elements used, topic, or mood. In this way, MLs remain engaged and also learn more about the possibilities for topic, elements, mood, and so on in their own digital stories. In the second sample worksheet, the topic of the story and the elements used are quite different. You will note that both sample worksheets use mostly multiple-choice questions. For MLs who have more language proficiency, short-answer or open-ended questions can also provide more challenge as they analyze the stories.

Sample worksheet for digital story (DS) analysis

DS Worksheet 2: My Story of Jing Di Zhi Wa

Digital Story by Xinyu (Amber) Wang, produced in Polina's class in spring 2022: https://youtu.be/ILds0KnCTRI
Directions: Watch Xinyu Wang's digital story and answer the questions.

1. What is the digital story about?
   a. The author's life in China
   b. Importance of exploring the world
   c. The author's travels around the world
2. Who is the digital story about?
   a. A frog in a well
   b. Students in the US
   c. The author's friends
   d. The author—Xinyu Wang
3. What elements do you see in this digital story?
   a. Pictures from the Internet
   b. Personal photos
   c. Animation
   d. Music
   e. Background music
   f. Gifs
   g. Drawings
   h. A person's voice
   i. Words on screen
   j. Videos
   k. ______________________
4. How many pictures do you see in this digital story?
   a. 45
   b. 12
   c. 31
   d. 23
5. How many video clips do you see in this digital story?
   a. 3
   b. 5
   c. 7
   d. 1
6. What languages did you hear or read in this story?
   a. English only
   b. Chinese only
   c. English and Chinese
7. What kind of music do you hear in this digital story?
   a. Calm and slow
   b. Loud and energizing
   c. Instrumental
   d. Dance music
8. How can you describe this digital story?
   a. Funny
   b. Interesting

   c. Boring
   d. Entertaining
9. How do you feel after watching this digital story?
   a. Happy
   b. Confused
   c. Sad
   d. Excited
10. Bonus! When did you first see an image of the author of the story? Why do you think the author first put her image then?

After MLs analyze two stories chosen by the teacher, we recommend having them find another story or two to watch on their own. This exercise further familiarizes MLs with the digital storytelling genre but also with the resources on digital storytelling that are available to them. We also want to incorporate choice to keep our MLs motivated and engaged in the process!

Language Skills and Choices

You no doubt will know a lot about your MLs' language levels with respect to the language you are teaching. MLs will need to use language for the following (and probably more!) functions as they create their digital story (see Table 5.1).

Practicing these language functions briefly before beginning the digital storytelling process is a good idea. You can also do short, five-minute mini lessons focused on one function to support MLs as they reach each stage. Providing sentence starters and examples of questions that MLs may want to ask can also support target language communication. Finally, encouraging dictionaries, electronic translators, and translanguaging can help all MLs communicate their thoughts and ideas to the best of their ability in whatever language they choose.

In addition to knowing MLs' target language abilities, you will also want to know what other languages and language features your MLs have in their linguistic repertoires. This helps you know what languages MLs could use in their stories, but it also helps MLs begin thinking about translanguaging in their stories. A good way to start is to have each ML create a language profile. You can give each ML a blank silhouette (or have them draw one) and then have them place all their languages on it, thinking about why they feel a certain part of their body corresponds to a certain language. You can see in Heather's example (Figure 5.1) that Spanish is in her heart as the language she chose to learn in high school and which she

Table 5.1 Language functions for digital storytelling work and collaboration

Language function	*DS step*	*Example*
Asking questions	Story circle	"Can you give any more detail about that experience?"
	Peer review	"Why did you use the present tense here?"
	Sharing of stories	"Was your family excited for you to tell this story?"
Asking for clarification	Peer review	"Can you tell me what you mean by ___?"
	Production	"I'm not sure I understand …"
Giving feedback (positive and negative)	Peer review	"I love how your images relate to the story."
	Sharing of stories	"I think you could have spent a little more time on the transitions between images."
Describing events	Story circle	"I want to tell my story about the first time I left my city. I was five years old …"
	Writing/recording the narrative	"I was five years old when I first traveled out of my city."
Problem solving	Production	"I don't know how to …"
Explaining	Peer review	"I chose this word because …"
	Production	"I need a transition that slowly changes from this image to the next."
	Sharing of stories	"My digital story is about …"
Evaluating	Final draft of verbal narrative	"I think this ending is best."
	Selecting images and music	"This one is better than the other because …"
	Peer review	"I think your images are clearer here than later on."
Brainstorming	Story circle	"My first idea was to talk about my hometown."
Encouraging	Peer review	"I know you can figure it out."

has spoken ever since. However, English is most represented in the profile because Heather lives and works in English-speaking environments all day every day. Chinese is in one hand and a foot because she learned a little for work, traveling to China with a group of students one summer. Portuguese is on the other hand as it is a language she is striving to learn, and French is also on that arm, as her sister speaks both languages. Finally, one leg is left mostly empty of language, signifying that Heather doesn't know yet what language she will add to her repertoire next and where it may take her! Color can also be used to communicate more information about how MLs feel about their different languages.

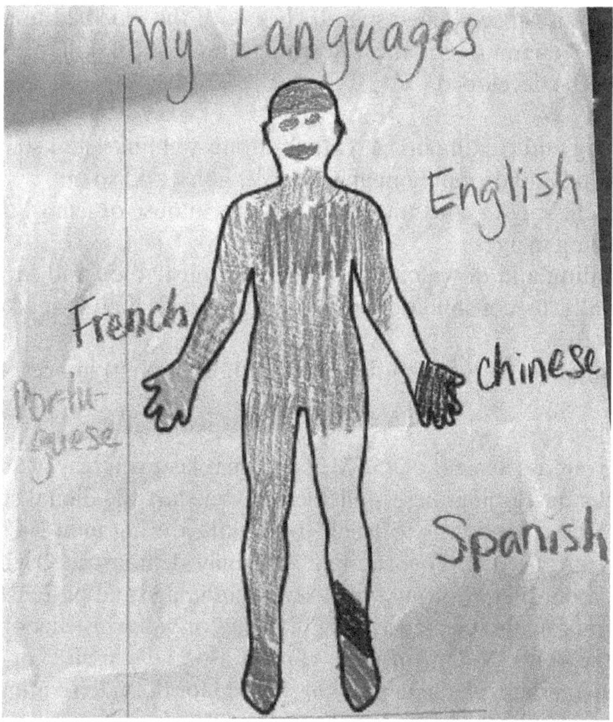

Figure 5.1 Heather's language profile. Image by Heather Linville.

Watch the digital story by an adult migrant, *From Guatemala to the USA*; https://www.youtube.com/watch?v=lcYjs35fcKo&t=62s. Think about how she uses Spanish and English to convey her message. This digital story is also a great example of how the creator uses a combination of still images and video clips to create a powerful, multimodal message. This digital story was produced in Carlye Stevens's class in summer 2022 (see also the featured digital storytelling project at the end of this chapter).

Skills for Digital Storytelling

MLs will need a wide range of technological and multimodal skills to create their best digital story. Skills are needed at each stage of the process as MLs craft their verbal narrative to be as engaging and economical as possible. They type the narrative to be easily read for recording, create a storyboard in which they match the verbal narrative to the images, expressively audio record the verbal narrative, find and collect visual images and music, identify and use special effects, and work with the video editing software you choose. At a minimum, the following technological skills are needed or will need to be developed:

- Copying and pasting images, attributions, weblinks, and so on
- Dragging and dropping images, words, links, and so on
- Right-clicking to copy and paste with the mouse or using "control c"
- Digitizing images
- Uploading and downloading images or music files, and saving them, especially to consolidate all images into one digital space for easy retrieval
- Resizing or otherwise editing (including cropping) images, videos, or music

Based on your assessment of the MLs in your class, you may want to spend a few weeks developing these skills before you start the digital storytelling project. Another option is to teach these skills during mini lessons at the point they are needed. For example, you may demonstrate right-clicking when storyboarding, showing how to copy an image and paste it into PowerPoint. You can also create written guidelines or video instructions to demonstrate the skills. Video tutorials can be especially useful for the more specific, and perhaps challenging, skills needed for the video editing software application you choose to use, an example of which was seen in Chapter 4.

Permission to Use Multimodal Elements

The final step in preparation with students is considering how they will get permission to use images or video clips or share images or video clips of other people, as well as the music they hope to use with their digital stories.

A note about using images and video clips

In general, using images will be easier in digital stories from an editing perspective versus using video clips. Depending on how tech savvy your MLs are, you may choose to limit them to only using still images, as we have done on occasion. On the other hand, if your MLs are tech savvy or tech curious and willing to learn, using a combination of still images and video clips can add another powerful layer of meaning in their digital stories. See this example of how an international student's story mixes still images and video clips: *Events that Gave Me Confidence*; https://youtu.be/LaklSvtVwnA. This digital story was produced as part of a class that Heather guest taught in fall 2021.

Permission to Use Images or Video Clips

The easiest way to use an image or video clip is to have MLs take the image or record the video themselves. MLs will not need permission to use their own digital media, and they can credit the images and video clips in their digital story by simply stating, "All images and videos are the author's own." However, if other people are included in the images or videos, such as friends or family members, MLs should get permission from those people to include the visuals in their story. Generally speaking, for educational purposes, an email exchange in which individuals in the images or videos give their permission is sufficient. If individuals do not give permission for their likeness to be used, MLs can either cut individuals out of the visuals or cover faces so the individuals are not recognizable.

Another option is to use Creative Commons (https://creativecommons.org/). Creative Commons has a vast database of images that are freely available to use, with proper crediting. Although it can be more difficult to find the exact image one wants to use, it is the best way to use images that you do not take yourself. Each Creative Commons image has information included on how to give credit to the author. For example, the image "World Map" Heather uses in her digital story would be credited as follows: "'World map' by Martyn Wright is licensed under CC BY 2.0. To view a copy of this license, visit https://creativecommons.org/licenses/by/2.0/?ref=openverse."

If MLs decide they need to use an image from the Internet, such as one they found through a Google search, they need to save the link and give the information in the credits at the end of the story. We suggest having students get in the habit of copying the link of each image as they save it. This can be done easily by pasting each potential image into a Word or Google document with the link underneath each image. Because the digital stories are only for educational purposes, it is permissible to copy and use images from the Internet, with proper crediting.

Permission to Use Music

The situation for using music in digital stories is similar. If your MLs have their own musical compositions, or create music using GarageBand or another application, they can use this music in their digital story without any restrictions. They can state in the credits, "Music is the author's own." However, to use commercially produced music, the situation is more complicated.

Creative Commons also has a vast database of songs that are freely available to use, with proper crediting. Creative Commons links to other databases, some of which require an account, and it can be challenging to weed through all the possible songs. As with images, each Creative Commons song has information included on how to give credit to the artist.

It is possible to use songs that MLs have downloaded from the Internet or even songs MLs own on CDs or in a digital music player because the digital stories are not made for any purpose beyond education. Nonetheless, MLs should give credit with the name of the composer and artist at the end of their digital story. However, when uploading these digital stories to YouTube, they could be flagged as including music for which you do not have permission to use. Additionally, if using the digital story later for other purposes beyond education, it would not be legal to have the song included. Therefore, we suggest using Creative Commons or having MLs produce their own background music.

Ready to Go!

You should now be feeling well prepared to begin your digital storytelling process! It is time to have MLs start thinking about the story that they would like to share. We suggest doing one or two brainstorming sessions during class. Here are a few ideas for brainstorming sessions:

- Free write—MLs write continuously for a certain amount of time (e.g., 3 minutes) to generate ideas
- Drawing—MLs create visual images about a story they want to tell
- Word web—MLs write a topic for their story and associated words
- Guided worksheet—specific questions about the story an ML might want to tell

MLs will always be at different stages in their idea development, and some may struggle to come up with an idea for a story they want to tell. For those MLs, you can have readymade themes, such as family, culture, or journeys (even a journey from elementary to middle school!), that MLs can choose from. This works especially well in conjunction with a word web, as shown in the example in Figure 5.2.

Digital story planning worksheet

Answer these questions about your digital story project.

1. What topic would you like to use for your digital story? Why do you want to explore that topic? Write a bit about your topic here.
2. How does your topic represent who you are?
3. What images do you plan to use in your digital story and why?
4. What music do you plan to use in your digital story and why?
5. What information/resources do you need to know in order to continue with this project?

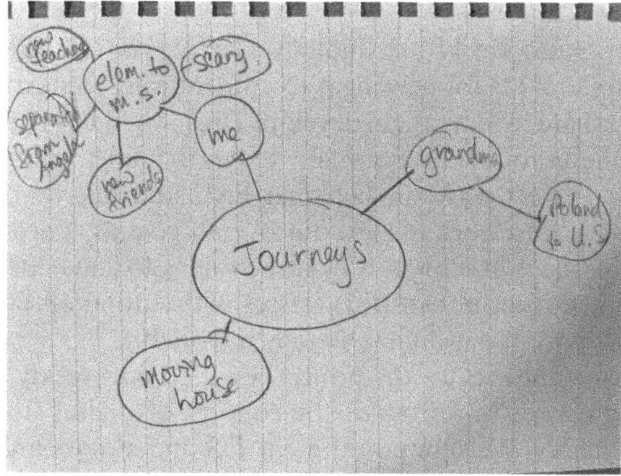

Figure 5.2 Word web brainstorming example. Image by Heather Linville.

In the featured digital storytelling project for this chapter, Debora Amidani and Carlye Stevens explain how they successfully implemented digital storytelling with what could be seen as several challenges. The MLs in their classes had limited English language skills, limited educational backgrounds, and low technological literacy. However, with good preparation and translanguaging, the MLs were successful in creating their own digital stories. A final note of encouragement: no digital storytelling project is ever perfect. You will forget to plan some piece, or how to do something in the application. Do not worry! We have made all the mistakes you will make, and we have survived and learned from them. Our MLs still produced amazing digital stories that they (and we) are immensely proud of! We know you will be able to do the same.

Featured digital storytelling project: Digital stories with adult beginner low literacy English language learners

Name: Debora Amidani and Carlye Stevens
Position: ESL Instructor (Debora) and Digital Literacy and Technology Instructor (Carlye), The Family Place Public Charter School
Project Location: Washington, DC, USA

The goal at The Family Place Public Charter School (TFPPCS) in Washington, DC, is to improve the literacy and workplace skills of adult immigrants so they can create a better life for themselves and their families. To help achieve this goal, we have an ESL program that incorporates weekly technology classes. As ESL instructors, we're always looking for new ideas to authentically contextualize the skills that we are helping them develop. Thus, when Dr. Polina Vinogradova (co-author of this book) invited us to implement this digital storytelling project with our beginner ESL students, we thought it was a great way to work toward our overall goal as educators. This project took place at TFPPCS from February to June 2022. We facilitated this project in two ESL classes with a total of 18 students and with help from our digital literacy instructors.

To prepare students for the project, we used our weekly one-hour technology classes to introduce the concept of digital stories (DS) and its elements. We showed different DS and storyboards to give examples of what students could create. By showing these examples, students felt more connected to the project and were excited to begin creating their own stories. The technology instructor also focused on developing students' digital skills such as using a computer mouse, adding and populating Google Slides, searching for images on Google, and using the video editing software PowerDirector.

The last two weeks of class, after standardized assessments, were completely devoted to DS work. It included scaffolded tasks for DS analysis and composing, multimodal drafting and feedback, and DS composing using PowerDirector video editing application for Chromebooks. As students created their DS, we encouraged them to use the languages they felt comfortable with. This promoted students' multilingual skills throughout the project. For example, students watched a multilingual DS produced in an ESL class at UMBC called "Real Men Do Housework" (https://www.youtube.com/watch?v=YT6cBfscybs&t=1s), created multilingual stories, and held multilingual discussions throughout the process of the project. Our expectations for the project varied based on the students' individual skills that they had demonstrated throughout the academic year. We wanted their stories to be personal so that it felt special to them and worth their time. At the end of the project, students created DS that covered a variety of topics: their English language learning journeys, home countries, lives in DC, families, and their own life histories.

The project concluded with our students presenting their DS to the other ESL classes and school staff. We were proud of the results and learned that this type of project is authentic, engaging, and exciting for students. We've noted that the audiences that watch these DS are touched by students' stories and thrilled to know that low-literacy ESL beginner students can deliver such a wonderful product. They understand how engaging this project is and how it piques students' interests. We've also noticed that many teachers want to implement this project in their classes but have some restraints like time and resources. For anyone who wants to undertake a similar project, we suggest teaching digital skills and exploring other DS as examples early on, letting students choose their own topics, and working on how to write a narrative from the beginning. Many of the digital stories created by TFPPCS students can be found on the school's website: https://www.thefamilyplacedc.org/digitalstorytellingeslclass.

Reference

Dörnyei, Z. (2018). *Engaging language learners in the 21st century* [PowerPoint slides]. TESOL International Convention Presentation. March 21, 2018.

6 Starting the Story

Story Circles and Writing the Narrative

Congratulations! Now you and your MLs are ready to begin the process of creating personal, engaging digital stories! In this chapter we will describe the first step, the story circle, and the process of writing a strong narrative. The story circle is the first opportunity MLs have to share their ideas for their digital stories, and therefore we focus heavily on the feedback from peers. The narrative guides and propels the digital story from the first moment and therefore is also crucial in the digital storytelling process. Let's get started!

Story Circles

Story circles are small groups of digital storytellers, sitting in a circle, orally sharing ideas for their digital stories one at a time. The primary goal of the story circle is to give creators their first opportunity for peer feedback. As each person speaks, their classmates listen and act as sounding boards to help them with their ideas. At this stage you will likely have MLs at various stages of idea development: MLs who have no idea the story they want to tell, MLs who have some ideas but need to clarify or focus their story, and MLs who have a very clear idea of their story and just need some support tweaking the story based on audience response. No matter where your MLs are in their process, they will all benefit from the story circle process. Note: If your MLs have not yet engaged in any sort of brainstorming or idea generation process for their digital story, we recommend you go back and do that before they engage in the story circle.

The Preparation

To start preparing your MLs for the story circle, let them know that each of them will be sharing their story ideas in small groups. Also let MLs know that you do not expect them to all have their stories completely figured out. Rather, the point of the story circle is to help them get more ideas, focus their story (or focus on one story if they are choosing between two or more ideas), discover what details they could add or remove, and if and how they need to modify their story idea based on how others respond.

DOI: 10.4324/9781003295730-8

It is especially important to reassure MLs that they still have plenty of time to write their narrative after the story circle.

> Heather remembers her first story circle and how helpful and enlightening it was in her own digital storytelling process. Heather came to the story circle with a very loose idea of the topic for her first digital story. She wanted to tell a story about the year she was an English Language Fellow in Indonesia and the challenges she faced. She also wanted to include many of the hundreds of pictures she had from her time there! However, as she told a story about one particularly challenging time in Indonesia, the other workshop participants asked questions only about the other person Heather was with in the story. Heather then realized the way she was telling her story was leading to confusion. She was able to clarify it to the other workshop participants, and then create a digital story that was clearer and a true representation of the message she wanted to share.

A good activity to prepare MLs is to do a mock story circle during which you share your story idea(s) and MLs give you feedback in the form of questions. This will model the process for MLs and build their confidence for sharing and being vulnerable with each other. You might talk about the challenges from a creator perspective. For example, you could mention how difficult it is to share an idea you are not sure about yet, but that you know you will get good feedback that will help you tell the best story you can. Be sure to instruct your MLs to ask questions in the story circle. One of the most important elements of digital storytelling is that the creator has complete control over the digital story. Therefore, it is necessary to have MLs practice asking questions of each other and avoiding statements. In the mock story circle, you can help MLs see the difference between telling a peer, "You should say … in your story" or "I think your story needs …" and asking a question, such as, "What other details could you add to the story?" or "What is the main idea you want to share in your story?" By asking questions, authors/creators see how they can clarify or change their stories to better communicate with the audience but they still have control over the process. In Table 6.1 we provide some suggested questions and feedback phrases that you can share with MLs to use in story circles.

To further prepare for the story circle activity, determine how you will divide MLs into smaller groups of five to eight MLs and which ML will be each group's leader. The group leader you choose needs to keep the group focused on the task, direct each ML when it is their turn to share, and ensure that peers are asking questions rather than making statements. You may want to talk to your group leaders separately to ensure they can handle the task.

Table 6.1 Sample language for story circles

Sample questions with the question words	*Sample feedback phrases*	*Sample language to support sharing digital story ideas*
• *Who* is the digital story about? Are you the main actor? • *What* is the main idea of the digital story that you want to share? • *When* did the event happen? What details about that time do you think you need to include? • *Where* did the event happen? Have you thought about images you could use to show the location? • *Why* do you want to share this story? What makes it important to you? • *How* do you think music will support your digital story? Have you thought about a song yet?	• This is a great story idea! I'm wondering … • The way you told your story really moved me. Have you thought about …? • I like your story idea. Could you provide some more details? • It's so great that you shared such a personal story. Are you worried about sharing it with the whole class or people beyond our class? • My favorite part of what you just said is …. What images do you think you will use to show it? • Thank you for sharing your story idea. Could you clarify … for me? • I can't wait to see your digital story. Have you thought about music yet?	• My idea for my story is …. • I want to create a digital story about the time … • I am trying to choose between two (or more) ideas. The first one is … • My story starts when I was … years old … • My story is really personal and hard to tell. • I hope you like the story idea I am going to share.

Working with young learners in the story circle

If you are working with MLs in elementary or primary school, you may find that it is too challenging for them to be group leaders. Rather, you may circulate the room yourself to ensure groups are on task, use a timer, direct all groups to move to the next person to share at certain times, and frequently use reminders about asking questions. If you have an aide in your classroom, you could lead two larger story circles.

It is important that all MLs feel supported during the story circle. To further prepare them, you can have MLs write down a few brief notes about their story idea. They can refer to this paper while sharing or for language or idea support and can take notes on the same sheet as they receive feedback from their peers. See Table 6.1 for some sentence starters MLs can use when sharing their story idea. Have these clearly visible in your classroom or have MLs write them on their note sheets. They can also translanguage to feel supported. We recommend encouraging MLs to use their full linguistic repertoire to share their ideas. This is the perfect time for MLs to be creative with language and try out explaining their story in different ways. Mixed language groups can work, or you may want to group MLs with similar language backgrounds into the same groups to facilitate this process.

Further prepare your MLs by letting them know that you will not be participating in a story circle but will be monitoring the class. This clearly communicates to your MLs that this is a different type of assignment and that they do not have to make a story that is pleasing to you, the teacher, or get your approval. Finally, prepare your classroom by moving desks out of the way, if possible, so MLs can face each other with nothing between them and their peers (See example in Figure 6.1.).

The Process

When you are ready to start the story circles, instruct your MLs to get into their pre-assigned groups and to bring their note sheets. Your group leaders in each group should start off by asking who wants to go first and asking that person to start speaking. If no one wants to go first, the group leader will probably have to begin. Be sure you have chosen group leaders who will be willing to do so! Group leaders will ensure that while each person has the floor (or is speaking), the others in the group listen and ask questions. The group leaders should also keep track of time and move on to the next person if the conversation goes on too long or becomes unproductive.

Let everyone know how long they have for the story circle (about five minutes per group member is usually enough time). If your groups need more or less time, be flexible. The important thing is that there is productive sharing, which is also building their language skills! If groups finish at different times, you can always have those that finish earlier move into the writing stage, which we explore in the next section.

At the end of the story circle, we suggest moving directly into writing the narrative while ideas are fresh in your MLs' minds. Having a strong narrative is an important next step in the digital storytelling process.

Writing the Narrative

Now that your MLs have engaged in the story circle, they are ready to write their narratives. Other genres, such as TikTok or other social media videos, are delivered using computer technologies and the web, so it is important to differentiate digital stories from these others. While other videos may be about marketing a product or sharing news or even humorous events with friends, digital stories are a medium for personal stories, which often explore critical moments in one's life. At their core, digital stories are just

Figure 6.1 Digital storytellers engaging in story circle. Photograph by Heather Linville.

stories told in a different format. Viewing a few other video genres for comparison might be helpful for your MLs to develop a clear idea of what you expect in their digital story.

Depending on your MLs' needs and your digital storytelling goals, you may need more or less teaching about narratives. For more advanced MLs, you will not need to spend much time on story structure or how to write a narrative, but you may have to remind them that they are telling a story. Advanced and not-so-advanced students can fall into the trap of writing about their home countries, cultural differences, or their lives without really telling a story. To be classified as a narrative, a text must have characters and objects in the plot, have a chain of events that influences the characters and objects and brings about changes, and it should be possible to interpret these events and thus understand the plot (Ryan, 2004). Narratives can differ in structure, content, social function, and organization and the goal of a narrative can be to amuse, inform, accuse, or argue for a particular point.

Digital stories are narratives that can have different structures and organization. They can be poetic or have dramatic qualities. While a number of digital stories and digital storytelling projects target social issues and are intentionally produced to challenge the social order, others are stories about family history or important events in people's lives. Whatever the purpose, all digital stories have plots with characters and objects in them influenced by events that are possible to interpret. These narrative qualities are present not only verbally, but also visually and musically. We will address this multimodal composing more in Chapter 7.

Digital stories' narratives tend to be nonfiction, condensed personal stories with a plot line. While chronological order is common in telling a story, narrative plots in digital stories can be developed in other ways, such as comparison/contrast, logical idea division, order of importance, or cause and effect. Another development is "consequential sequencing" (Kohler Riessman, 1993, p. 17), which orders events in the plot without reference to a time frame. It is important to note that what is considered "logical" development in a story is culturally bound. For MLs who have grown up writing in other cultures, it can be worthwhile to compare and contrast typical logical ordering in writing styles in English with those of other cultures. MLs can be encouraged to seek out and use other ordering in their stories that they find logical. This is another way to maximize translanguaging in digital stories. Digital stories can also be very entertaining, as any story can be.

A good activity for MLs before they start writing their own narrative is to analyze another digital story's narrative. This activity can help them identify the essential elements of a narrative (characters/objects, plot, chain of events that impact the characters/objects) as well as see an example of how the elements can be presented in a story. Providing the written narrative is especially helpful for MLs to see and analyze the author's rhetorical moves, or how she developed her story. We offer an example in the box.

Narrative analysis worksheet: A Good (Hmong) Woman

Digital Story by Kazoua Yang, produced in Heather's class in spring 2022: https://youtu.be/aOGYcDhxPgs

Part 1:

Watch the story once. Then read the digital story script as you watch the story again.

I am a good Hmong woman. My mom and dad raised me to be a good Hmong daughter. My mom and dad taught me to be a good Hmong wife. My mom and dad showed me to be a good Hmong daughter-in-law. What does it even mean?

A good Hmong daughter does whatever her mom and dad say. Mom and dad say, "You cannot speak up, girls can never do that." She nods. Mom and dad say, "You are a girl, you cannot play sports." A good Hmong daughter says, "Um," which means OK in Hmong. A good Hmong wife does whatever her husband desires. Her husband says,

"You cannot have friends anymore because you are now married." She says, "Um." Her husband says, "I want ten kids." A good Hmong wife says, "Um." A good Hmong wife does whatever her in-laws and the elders want. Her in-laws say, "You need to wake up at 4 am in the morning and cook breakfast for everyone." She does it. The elders say, "It's never our son's fault." A good daughter-in-law says, "Um."

I am not a good Hmong daughter. I spoke up, especially when my mom and dad said only boys can play volleyball. I went to play volleyball. I am not a good Hmong wife, I kept friends, both men and women. And I told my husband, I did not want ten kids. I am not a good Hmong daughter-in-law. I slept in until 7 am because I worked late the night before, and I told the elders, sometimes it is your son's fault. What a bad Hmong woman, huh?

I don't think so! I think I am a good woman. My mom and dad raised me to be a good daughter. I speak up for myself, for them, and the people around me. I show them that I can succeed, even in sports. I was good at volleyball and have won many tournaments. My mom and dad taught me to be a good wife. I have a diverse group of friends, men and women, gays and lesbians, Blacks, Whites, and Samoan. I have two children and I only want four. My mom and dad showed me to be a good daughter-in-law. I get up early and make breakfast when I can. And of course if it is their son's fault, I am going to say that, but if it is my fault, I will own it. My daughter is a Hmong young woman. I will raise, teach, and show her how to be a good woman.

Part 2:

Answer these questions based on what you've seen and read.

1. Highlight/circle all personal pronouns you see in this script. What personal pronouns does the author use?
2. What makes this story personal?
3. What makes this story interesting?
4. How does the author use multiple languages?
5. How does the author organize her story? Choose one:
   a. Chronologically
   b. Order of importance
   c. Comparison/contrast
   d. Cause and effect
   e. Consequential sequencing
6. What captures your attention in this story?
7. What did you learn about family, community, and belonging from this story?

Once you feel your MLs have a good grasp on how to write a narrative, they are ready to take the feedback from the story circle and get started! Since many of us have a hard time facing a blank page, we suggest using a graphic organizer to help MLs begin writing. A simple online search using the terms "writing narrative graphic organizer" will lead to many examples appropriate for the age and language level of your MLs. They range from just a list of question words (*who*, *what*, *when*, *where*, *why*, *how*) with blanks for MLs to fill in their answers, to more complicated structures asking for character(s), setting, problem, solution, and notes on the beginning, middle, and end of the story. If MLs have a graphic organizer they are used to, for example from their other academic work or classes, we suggest using the same one for their digital story narrative. Sticky notes, as suggested by Lambert (2009), or the virtual version, Padlet (https://padlet.com), can also be used to help MLs organize their thoughts as they create their narrative. An additional advantage of Padlet is that MLs can add images, their own or from the Internet, that they are considering using in their digital stories to help them in their thought process. Later, when they are mapping their multimodal narratives and developing digital story maps (see Chapter 7), they will be able to reuse these images, adding more or deleting them, depending on the development of their multimodal thought process.

You may want MLs to collaborate as they work on their narratives, or you may encourage them to work alone. No matter your classroom style, do not forget to encourage and expect translanguaging at this stage. There is no rule that a narrative should be written all in one language. Rather, MLs can use all their languages/language features to express their ideas in the most complete and accurate way. Having full access to all their linguistic resources will help tremendously as MLs begin to consider the best ways to share their stories.

You may have MLs that struggle to come up with a draft at this point. However, even at this early point it is necessary for each ML to have a draft of their narrative in order to go on to the next stages. It may be helpful to have a deadline for the draft and allow class time to ensure everyone can complete it. Once a draft is complete, you may want to have MLs engage in peer collaboration for feedback on their narrative (see more in Chapter 9). While not essential, we have found that MLs appreciate another person reading their story and giving feedback before they go onto the next stage. The following box provides an example of a peer feedback sheet. You may note the focus on the future audience of the story here and in the preceding narrative analysis example. By asking questions about what makes the story interesting or what captures the audience's attention, we are reminding authors to keep their audience in mind at all times. Many graphic organizers will also ask what is the "hook", or engaging opener, that will grab the audience's attention. At the end of the day, a digital story that doesn't care about its audience will not have much of an audience to view it.

Digital storytelling narrative peer feedback questions

1. How did/could your partner's story grab your attention at the beginning?
2. Is it a personal story about your partner? If not, who or what is the main character in the story?
3. What is the problem to be solved or other tension explored in the story?
4. How does your partner explain the emotion in the story?
5. How does the language(s) your partner uses in the story add interest or information?
6. Does the story seem like it is too short or too long?
7. What music do you imagine hearing with this story?
8. What images do you hope to see with this story?

In the following featured digital storytelling project, Tamara Mae Roose used a digital storytelling project to develop MLs' reading and writing skills in her first-year writing course. She discusses how she used readings to help MLs to explore gender, language, and cultural identities. After MLs wrote their own narratives about a memorable moment in their lives related to their language and cultural identity, they created their digital stories. In this way, the writing of the digital story narrative directly supports MLs' academic writing skills.

In this chapter, we have explored the first stages of digital story production—utilizing the story circle and crafting the written narrative. The next chapters bring in the real fun of digital storytelling with multimodal composing. While you may still be convincing MLs of the worthwhileness of this project, now that the drafts are written, the mood in the classroom may shift. We find at this point that most MLs are eager to discover more about each other as they hear about and give feedback on each other's stories. They also become excited about envisioning their own digital stories, ready to find the images and music they will use to portray their stories in their digital multimodal composition. They also might be getting nervous, knowing that their technological skills will be in high demand over the next stages. Whatever the mood in your classroom, we are excited for you as you lead your learners through this process! It only gets better from here ….

Featured digital storytelling project: Reflections on my language and culture identity

Name: Tamara Mae Roose
Position: Assistant Professor of TESOL, Department of Teacher Education and Foundations, California State University, San Bernardino, San Bernardino, California, USA
Project Location: Dobbs Ferry, New York, USA

I remember the first time my abuela called me a "sin vergüenza." I was nine years old. When she said it, I was really confused because I knew it as a negative thing. But when my abuela calls me a "sin vergüenza," she means I am fearless.

In my first-year writing (FYW) courses at Mercy College, a Hispanic-Serving institution in New York where I previously worked, I taught predominantly generation 1.5 multilingual college students from diverse language and culture backgrounds. Many of their families came to the United States from Puerto Rico and the Dominican Republic, with individuals from El Salvador, Ghana, Guatemala, Guinea, Haiti, India, Ivory Coast, Jamaica, Mexico, Senegal, and Uruguay. Some students immigrated during elementary or secondary school, while most were born in the United States but grew up speaking languages other than English at home and in their communities.

In fall 2022, across four sections of the course offered in-person and online, we explored gender, language, and culture identity by engaging with reading texts from diverse authors. A major assignment was a personal narrative project aimed at increasing students' understanding of genre, point of view, audience awareness, and use of different rhetorical appeals. The goal was for students to explore a memorable event in their lives that tells a story about their language and culture identity. Across the first few weeks, we discussed Sandra Cisneros' "Only Daughter," Gloria Anzaldúa's "How to Tame a Wild Tongue," and Amy Tan's "Mother Tongue." As modeled by these authors, students then wrote their own personal narratives where they applied what they learned about the genre (e.g., use of vivid description, sensory details, first-person perspective, rich dialogue, flashbacks, etc.) and incorporated different languages and Englishes in their stories. Students later returned to these narratives as the culminating project by showcasing them as digital stories during the final class session, using Microsoft PowerPoint as our video editing software.

In this personal narrative project, students' cultural and linguistic backgrounds were positioned as central to their academic literacy development as multilingual college writers. Powerful stories emerged foregrounding students' lived experiences as children of immigrant families, such as language learning, translating for family members, visiting parents' homeland, facing language oppression and racial discrimination, grieving family illness, incarceration, and loss, and dealing with domestic violence and financial struggles.

Here are some sample narratives from some of the digital stories from this project.

> During our stay in Mexico, we were woken up by the roosters each morning, or as we call it, *el canto de los gallos*, roosters singing. I was not an early bird back then, but hearing the roosters was more than enough to be awake each morning. The lifestyle from Mexico was so different from what I was used to back in New York … from sitting on the back of a pick-up while in motion to having wildlife as close as your backyard.

> When the teacher pointed at a poster on the wall, the entire class yelled "APPLE." In my head, I couldn't help but think, "No, eso es una manzana." And in the moment, I decided to raise my hand and speak the only language I knew. All I heard was the universal sound of laughter.

> "Nana, que pasa. Por favor dime que estás bien," I said with tears streaming down my face. 12/08/14 was the worst day of my life. Nana, who is my grandma, is my best friend, the most loving, compassionate, strong, hot-headed person I know. She left her hometown Santiago De Los Caballeros, Dominican Republic at the age of 22, leaving behind an infant daughter, so she could jump-start her life in the US. Leaving her daughter was one of the hardest decisions of her life, but she knew it needed to be done for her to have a better life.

The act of telling and listening to stories—having a voice and feeling heard—ultimately helped establish a stronger classroom community where students exhibited increased confidence, communication, and connection. I was surprised by how engaged students were in each step of the project—from drafting their narratives to providing peer review to one another to showcasing them to the class. Some students were initially hesitant and expressed fear of social judgment from peers, so we established ground rules on the board together to unpack how we would honor and respect one another's stories before sharing them. Those who seemed most resistant initially were the most vocal about the meaningfulness of the project at the end. For example, students were each required to provide peer review to two classmates, but one student exclaimed aloud on his way out of the classroom, "Can I read *all* of them?! These are powerful!" Another student in an online break-out room shared, "Y'all have had hard lives, not just me.... Never thought I'd get to write about my own life in college."

Writing personal narratives is a common assignment within many FYW courses, and I hope more educators will use this opportunity to not only encourage students to draw upon their diverse language and cultural backgrounds but also meaningfully scaffold this into projects to model how to do so.

References

Kohler Riessman, C. (1993). *Narrative analysis*. Sage Publications.

Lambert, J. (2009). *Digital storytelling: Capturing lives, creating community* (3rd ed.). Digital Diner Press.

Ryan, M.-L. (2004). Introduction. In M.-L. Ryan (Ed.), *Narrative across media: The language of storytelling* (pp. 1–40). University of Nebraska Press.

7 Mapping the Multimodal Narrative

After all of the interactive work of brainstorming, giving feedback, writing narratives, and thinking about and selecting multimodal components, MLs are ready to map their digital stories. This stage includes storyboarding, recording the audio narrative, and organizing all the multimodal components. For your MLs, this is the stage in which they start to see their digital stories take shape. In this chapter, we explain the digital literacy skills that are necessary for digital storytelling projects. These skills are useful for all MLs given the importance of digital literacies today. As highlighted in Chapter 4, these skills include multimodal ways to create meaning and critical understanding of this meaning developed in interactions with others.

Storyboarding and Multimodal Composing

Storyboarding entails putting together the multimodal components of digital stories and organizing them on paper or in a digital storyboard. Beyond technological skills, multimodal composing skills are also essential for digital storytelling. In multimodal composing, MLs need to be aware of the visual, textual, and auditory elements and how each of them combine and support each other to produce a coherent digital story. MLs are used to writing in school to display their knowledge and complete tasks, with the occasional oral presentation. In a multimodal composing assignment, such as a digital storytelling project, MLs need to learn that the written/spoken text doesn't have to carry all the meaning. Rather, a picture can say a thousand words and reduce what needs to be said in the voiceover. In addition, the music can serve as background, setting the mood or tone of the piece, or it can be a part of the story.

> Watch the digital story *Here!* by Deya Ortiz; https://youtu.be/aavW3Tzt58c. Notice how the music changes as the creator, an adult migrant, moves. This story was produced in Heather and Polina's workshop in summer 2022.

DOI: 10.4324/9781003295730-9

Lambert and Hessler (2018) see a storyboard as a

> place to plan out a visual story in two dimensions. The first dimension is time: what happens first, next, and last. The second is interaction: how the audio - the voiceover narrative of your story and the music - interact with the images or video.
>
> (p. 115)

In this way, MLs begin to envision how the multiple elements of their digital story will come together. The storyboarding process also gives MLs the opportunity to think about possible video and sound effects, the use of additional text or animation, and the levels of the sound and various other multimodal emphasis that can be added to the story. The storyboard should include six components: images, visual effects, transitions, voiceover, soundtrack, and special effects.

In our work, we like to use PowerPoint or Google Slides (in Google Drive) as an interactive and less linear way to map out and organize digital story components. The various multimodal features of PowerPoint and Google Slides allow MLs to group several visuals and chunks of text onto one slide. In this way, they can see a more complete picture of how multimodal elements will interact with each other. They can also add some special effects and animation to the slides, add notes on music, and assess whether they have enough visuals for their projects. Another useful feature is the ability to zoom out to see the whole slide deck together and get a full picture of how their digital story is shaping up.

A storyboard can also be organized in a table, such as seen in Table 7.1. In low-tech teaching contexts, or with MLs who have lower technological literacy, such a storyboard template is useful to guide digital story creators in the storyboarding process. This format is particularly useful for MLs who are using a limited number of images. It also allows MLs to organize the layers of images, effects, voiceover, and soundtrack in a rather linear format, giving them a clear idea of how their digital story is coming along in terms of what elements they already have and what other elements might be needed. When using a large number of images, a table might get too long and crowded, which is not going to be helpful in providing a clear multimodal layout of the storyboard. Lambert and Hessler (2018, pp. 118–119) provide other examples of storyboards.

As MLs are organizing their multimodal components, whether in a table, in PowerPoint, or Google Slides, they start viewing their digital story as a whole. Perhaps for the first time in the digital storytelling process, they see how their story might be conveyed with all the multimodal elements and nuances they have so far. Seeing the big picture can help MLs identify whether they need to adjust, replace, or find more visuals; whether they still need to make any changes to their verbal narratives (e.g., incorporate the home language, adjust pitch, intonation, pacing, and emphasis); and

Table 7.1 Template for storyboard, adapted from Lambert and Hessler (2018)

Images	In each box, insert an image, groups of images, or their description					
Visual Effects	e.g., fade-in/ fade-out					
Transitions	e.g., cross- dissolve					
Voiceover	Excerpts from the narrative					
Soundtrack	Notes on music					
Special Effects	E.g., text over image, sound effects, animation					

whether they would like to use various additional multimodal elements and special effects. Some storyboards might look incomplete. These gaps in the storyboard are likely to reflect the thought process and realization that the author needs more elements or different elements to add to their multimodal narrative. At this stage, they can also identify music and think more about the meaning it adds to their digital story.

Translanguaging in Storyboarding

At this stage of digital multimodal composing, MLs can think more about the use of various languages in their stories, both orally and visually. For example, if they are reporting on conversations with family members or friends in which they would naturally use their home language or multiple languages, they can be encouraged to reflect this in their script and storyboard with translanguaging. In our experience, MLs can be concerned how audience members (including their instructors) will understand their digital stories if they use languages other than English. In response, we encourage MLs to think about how they can utilize multimodality, including the use of text on screen (i.e., subtitles), to address their concerns.

The storyboard example in Figure 7.1 is a good illustration of translanguaging in a digital story. You can see that the ML chose to use Spanish when focusing on their home country of El Salvador and switched to English when talking about their new life in the United States. In the earlier versions of this ML's storyboard, they used more Spanish to brainstorm the narrative and had fewer images.

> Watch the digital story *I am American, but…*; https://www.youtube.com/watch?v=8LUZBhPjb8c as an example to discuss with MLs various options with translanguaging. This digital story was produced in Heather's class in spring 2022.

Collaboration and Storyboarding

Storyboarding can also be another opportunity for student collaboration, reflection, and peer feedback. Here we provide some brief information on how to have MLs peer-review each other's storyboards. As you plan to have MLs collaborate and give each other feedback, you may want to revisit Table 5.1 in Chapter 5 and go over expressions and phrases useful for this type of work. MLs can also do this peer review with a focus on translanguaging. For example, you can ask MLs to identify places in their and their partner's storyboard where it would be appropriate to bring in their home languages or other languages relevant to their narratives. If they share a common home language, they can do peer review in this language to facilitate translanguaging and further understand how multiple

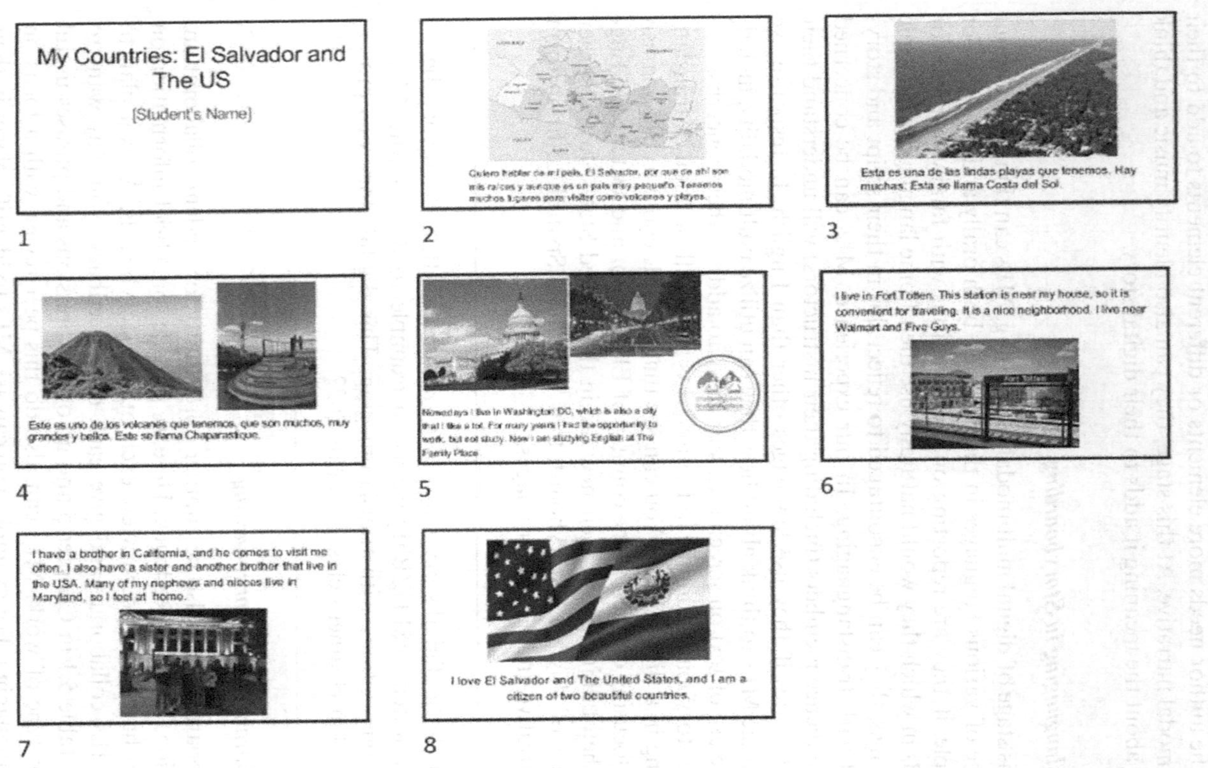

Figure 7.1 Google Slides for the digital story *My Countries: El Salvador and the US* created as part of the brainstorming–storyboarding–narrative development process in Debora Amidani's class (see featured digital storytelling project in Chapter 5).

languages can add to multimodal meaning in their digital stories. This is another way to create space for MLs' authentic language practices and voices and encourage them to employ their full linguistic and multimodal repertoires. Chapter 9 includes more information and sample peer feedback forms that include translanguaging.

Another Option: Storyboarding as the Starting Point of a Digital Storytelling Project

When we look at traditional sequencing of the steps in digital storytelling projects, we find digital storyboarding after brainstorming, writing the verbal narrative, and collecting visuals. It is step eight of the digital storytelling process in Table 2.1. However, this is not a prescribed order. You may choose to have your MLs use storyboarding as part of their brainstorming process. Polina has used this approach and found it particularly useful with MLs who have low technological literacy skills or have limited or no experience putting together presentations in PowerPoint or Google Slides.

If you choose to start with the storyboard, have MLs open a new PowerPoint or Google Slides document and start making notes about their stories on the slides in any language they choose to use. At the same time, encourage MLs to browse images and videos they have stored on their phones, go out and take new pictures or videos, or search Google Images for appropriate visuals while thinking about the message they are trying to create. Then, they can return to their slides to revise and further write their verbal narratives, continue working on their visuals, and start thinking about music.

Starting the digital storytelling process with the storyboard can help MLs envision their digital stories as a multimodal narrative from the very beginning. This can be particularly helpful for MLs who have never done multimodal projects like this before. MLs with low levels of technological literacy skills can get more and more familiar with one form of technology—PowerPoint or Google Slides—and develop their technological literacy in a focused way without being introduced to multiple forms of technology at the same time. While still complicated, as MLs have to learn to use and manipulate the mouse; develop and sequence slides; type in text fields; search for and arrange images; and copy/paste in the context of one application, it can be more productive and less intimidating for some MLs as they gradually get more and more comfortable with technology. They are able to pay more attention to the content of their digital stories rather than being worried about correctly operating a computer as PowerPoint or Google Slides become the main application for brainstorming, storyboarding, and developing their multimodal narratives (see Figure 7.1). This cyclical process of composing, assessing, and revising is also particularly helpful for MLs of lower levels of English language proficiency as they can focus more on the multimodal composing process and overall message of their digital stories.

To illustrate this point, we share here Polina's experience with the ML whose storyboard is featured in Figure 7.1. Polina closely observed her as she went through the multimodal composing process over a period of four days. During this time, the ML wrote two drafts of the verbal narrative in her notebook, gradually transitioning from a narrative in Spanish to expanding the use of English. She was empowered to do so on her own, at home, with the help of an online translator, without being prompted by her instructor. As her narrative grew, she realized the need to look for more images. Here, Polina prompted her to see if she had any personal images she would like to include, and the ML found several (See Figure 7.1, slides 4 and 7). She searched for other images using Google Images. Working in Google Slides from the very beginning of the project allowed this ML to get comfortable with a previously unfamiliar application and use it continuously for the purposes of brainstorming, composing, and revising her digital story. She was able to see her multimodal narrative shaping up gradually and assess if any other elements were necessary.

Recording the Narrative

Once storyboarding is complete, it is time for MLs to audio record their verbal narratives. If they wrote the narrative on paper, in a Google Doc, or in a Word document, they can work with this document to prepare for recording. If, however, they used PowerPoint or Google Slides to compose their narrative, such as on the slides or in the notes section, they will need to copy and paste the narrative into a Google Doc or a Word document to make it easier to read while recording. For MLs with lower technological literacy skills, this becomes yet another useful exercise in copying and pasting and arranging their narrative in paragraphs and meaningful chunks of text.

For all MLs, it is useful to think about how they will be reading their narratives. The text on the page should be large enough to make it easy to read and follow the lines. We recommend that the document be printed or read from a large screen rather than reading from a smartphone screen, which can be difficult. Printing the document before recording the narrative has two additional advantages:

1. MLs can annotate their document to indicate pauses, intonation, pitch, increase and decrease in the volume of voice, and meaningful connections. This is a great way to work with MLs on suprasegmental features in their narrative as they can think about how these features can contribute to the power of their message.
2. MLs will not need to worry about scrolling down the text on screen as they read, they can have the page close to them, and they can use a ruler or another device to follow the lines.

Be sure to remind MLs that all noises around them or those that they make will get recorded. For example, noise from a squeaky chair, flipped pages, and a mouse and keyboard often make it into the recording, resulting in the need to re-record their narrative. For this reason, we also recommend that the narrative document be printed on one side of paper to avoid the sound of flipped pages in the recording. At the same time, you can let MLs know that the recording does not have to be perfect. Pauses that are too long, coughing, or word repetitions can be edited and fixed when MLs start working with video editing software.

When MLs are ready to record their verbal narratives, we recommend finding a quiet space, perhaps a separate classroom, to record. MLs can use their smartphones' voice recording application (e.g., Voice Memos on iPhone) and headphones to record. Of course, it is helpful if your school or program has access to high quality audio recording equipment or at least a good microphone. If you have it, use it. At the same time, in our work, we have found that while professional grade equipment is nice to have, it is not essential for recording good quality sound.

Organizing Multimodal Components

Once you have reached the storyboarding stage of your digital storytelling project and have the narrative audio recorded, it is important to guide the MLs in organizing their multimodal components. This can become a part of digital literacies development where MLs think about the power of multimodality, the multimodal message they want to convey, and the audience for their message. This will also make working with multimodal elements easier, especially since from this point on, the number of components and pieces will start growing and changing. Keeping them organized and clearly labeled will make the process of multimodal composing, drafting, and redrafting much easier and less confusing and frustrating. We recommend using Google Drive for organizing the components, as mentioned in Chapter 4. At this point, you also need to instruct MLs to back up their work.

> As stated in Chapter 4, we recommend using Google Drive for digital storytelling work for multiple reasons. First, MLs can use their existing Gmail addresses and create a separate project folder. If MLs don't have a Gmail address, this is a good time to set up one to use for class and personal purposes. Many schools use Google Classroom, a program which includes the use of Gmail and Google Drive. By continuing to use Google Drive, you can avoid adding yet another new technology and log-in to MLs' technology repertoires.

Whether using Google Drive or organizing files on the computer drive or in the cloud, we suggest MLs set up a digital story project folder with the following subfolders: (1) verbal narrative, (2) visuals, (3) music, and (4) special effects. We also recommend developing a labeling system that is easy to follow and understand, such as "Safa Verbal Narrative 1" for the first recording of the narrative, or "Safa Image 3" for the image Safa wants to use third in her digital story. Labeling in an organized manner will be very helpful when importing multimodal narrative components into the video editing software and then building the digital story timeline in the software interface. When your MLs are organizing their multimodal narrative components, you may have to deal with the following:

1. Some MLs will decide to re-record their verbal narratives or parts of their narratives and, as a result, will have multiple audio files for their narrative to use when working with the video editing software.
2. Some MLs will decide to adjust, change, or add to their visuals, add special effects, and further revise their visuals.
3. MLs will continue working on selecting their music and some might choose to use several music files to add to their digital stories.
4. MLs might look to develop gifs, incorporate cartoons, or add various special effects to their visuals.

This continuous multimodal work will result in the accumulation of multiple files, some of which MLs will see as not needed anymore and some not originally included in the storyboard will be added at this point. For this reason, careful organization of files and clear labeling is an important aspect of multimodal composing and management of the components. We suggest advising MLs against deleting old files and instead having a separate folder for them. This way, if they change their minds, they will still have the files and can easily incorporate them back into their digital stories.

Even with all of the potential challenges, we find this stage of the digital storytelling process highly enjoyable. MLs think deeply and interact enthusiastically with each other and us as they make choices about which visuals and music to use. This learning process is a joy to watch.

In the following featured digital storytelling project, Andrea Lypka explains how she encouraged multimodal understanding in her project with international university MLs. It offers a clear example of how multimodal components can be mapped into a simplified academic digital storytelling project. She also provides details on how she prepares her MLs for this task, which requires new skills most of them have not yet developed.

At this point, we would like to say *Congratulations*!!! to you and your MLs. You have done a substantial amount of work and completed the first ten stages of your digital story projects (revisit Table 2.1 to see your progress)! Your MLs have developed and organized all of their multimodal narrative components and you all are now ready to move to the production stage of digital stories using video editing software. The next chapter will guide you through the exciting process of digital multimodal composing.

Featured digital storytelling project: Through our lens: Student perspectives about navigating identities in academia through student-created visual texts

Name: Andrea Enikő Lypka
Position: Adjunct English for Academic Purposes Instructor, University of South Florida
Project Location: Tampa, Florida, USA

In order to encourage a sense of belonging, provide a choice of expression, and to encourage students to take charge of their learning, I combined participatory photography, storytelling, technology, and project-based, reflective learning in the redesign of my English for Academic Purposes course, *English for International Students I*. (Please also see Lypka, 2020 and Lypka & De Felice, 2020 for more on this work.) The purpose of this course was to help advanced-level students continue to develop academic skills needed for university study while learning about the content areas of immigration and globalization. I also wanted to equip students with skills to use mobile phone cameras to foster a school-community relationship and an environment of self-expression, consistency, and familiarity through the course. The 15 first-year graduate students in the course came from Bahrain, China, Oman, and Saudi Arabia to study engineering, health sciences, and microbiology in the United States.

In the class, I implemented a simplified version of digital storytelling, student-created visual texts (SVTs), coupled with a process of interpretation and reflection to achieve several goals. First, I wanted to connect classroom learning with students' personal experiences and to evoke deeper understanding of how they navigate belonging in higher education, including relationships with faculty, access to and awareness of available services, communities on campus and beyond, and their existing relationships. I also wanted students to hone their visual presentation, research, writing, and reading skills as well as their teamwork and cooperation skills. The final goal was for learners to use mobile phones and computer-based tools to represent their stories using graphics, audio, drawings, video, and web publishing.

To prepare students for the task, I first asked them to choose a phrase, metaphor, or concept that best captured their experiences learning English (e.g., "Learning English is like ..."). For example, one student said, "Learning English is like conversion my brain from right to left. We have different structure in our native language in grammar and writing, we start from the right, and the sentences begin with verb and then subject." This task made apparent that, even though the students were proficient English speakers, they struggled with anxiety in interactions with other English speakers, engaging in research, and producing academic presentations. To work through these anxieties, students explored how they could use digital storytelling to document their experiences. I encouraged students to explore their world as they take photographs or videos and then use these visuals as catalysts for verbal and written expression. I also encouraged them to share ideas in their home language. I had them take five pictures to discuss in class and modeled for students how to read visual texts (i.e., photographs, maps, cartoons) related to the course content.

These two preparatory activities and the use of examples from previous SVT projects reinforced familiarity with the method; students were now ready to produce their SVTs. They were tasked with visually representing some aspect of immigration or globalization in their surroundings at the university. The students could create and represent meaning in any linguistic mode (e.g., they could translate vocabulary and share their projects with friends and family to comment on the project; they also had the option to interview others and translate the content as a voiceover), using diverse formats (e.g., a multimedia book, video, or skit) and platforms (e.g., Animoto, Canva, or Google Slides for presentations, Fliphtml5 for bookmaking, Powtoon, PowerPoint, Prezi, Storyjumper). Finally, students presented their SVT to their peers; they interpreted one image by explaining their intentions for capturing the visual and their understanding of what it represents. Students appreciated the questions and constructive feedback following the presentations. They were very engaged in these presentations because they felt a strong emotional connection to the content and enjoyed telling stories about different cultures on campus and beyond.

After the project, students submitted written reflections about the SVTs, including their perception of their performance on the task. Their reflections revealed that the SVTs helped improve their observation, critical thinking, and learning skills. More importantly, it helped them understand the underlying meanings of visuals, appreciate different perspectives, and connect with future goals and other courses. While print-based communication remains a primary teaching strategy in higher education, multimodal projects expand meaning-making potential. The SVT task required students to exercise agency over the topic and engage in creative multimodal communication strategies through combining visual, written, oral, and digital modes without the sophisticated editing and use of voiceovers and storyboards. While students often use multimodal communication outside the class, for many students in this course the SVT assignment was a first to ask them to integrate multimodal communication into their coursework to aid comprehension of key concepts and reflect on their learning. Storytelling and reflective practice contributed to developing a professional student identity. Students were able to grapple with the idea that identities can be multiple, fluid, and overlapping.

Figure 7.2 provides an example of a student-created image and reflection. It illustrates the ways in which digital storytelling and reflective literacy practices not only provide students opportunities to share their voices but to improve English skills through digital image composing and uploading, reflective writing, presenting, asking questions during presentations, and providing feedback on presentations. For example, the author of the self-portrait (Figure 7.2) examined how the smoking ban on campus interfered with international students' socializing activities. The student's reflection reveals his choice to focus on the new smoke-free policies on campus: "The picture is a self-portrait: I am smoking beside a no-smoking sign at the library. This picture from my daily life helped me to present about immigrations and problems some immigrants are facing. And I could directly relate that picture to [course reading] which says most Americans who disagree with the immigration movement are saying that immigrants

Figure 7.2 Example of student-created self-portrait with written reflection by the student author. Image by the student.

bring their bad habits from their countries to the U.S." In the presentation the student explained that using tobacco allowed him to reduce anxiety and connect with fellow international students on campus. The student mentioned that on one hand smoking had health hazards, but the smoke-free policies infringed on his individual freedom to use tobacco. The class discussion following the presentation prompted this student to focus his final research project on international students' perceptions of the smoking ban on campus.

The student-generated visual texts coupled with a process of interpretation, presentation, and reflection can help mitigate formulaic academic tasks, enable students to take on active roles, and spark alternative, creative, and refreshing ways to connect the course content to lived experiences. Yet student mixed media projects are underused with multilingual students to elicit their understanding and critical interpretation. Ultimately, in sharing my experiences with a simplified version of digital storytelling task and example projects, I invite you to experiment with student-authored multimedia techniques as a means towards a more personal, student-centered, and inquiry-based praxis across teaching contexts and proficiency levels.

References

Lypka, A. (2020). Digital storytelling with video voice. In *Digital literacy framework for adult learners: Instructor implementation guide* (pp. 7–10). Maryland Department of Labor's Adult Education. Retrieved from https://www.dllr.state.md.us/gedmd/dlfinstructorguide.pdf

Lypka, A. E., & De Felice, D. (2020). Telecollaborative storytelling: Reframing language learners' and preservice teachers' identity, multimodal literacy, and intercultural competency through telecollaborative digital storytelling. In G. Neokleous, A. Krulatz, & R. Farrelly (Eds.), *Handbook of research on cultivating literacy in diverse and multilingual classrooms* (pp. 146–165), IGI Global. doi: 10.4018/978-1-7998-2722-1.ch008

Reference

Lambert, J., & Hessler, B. (2018). *Digital storytelling: Capturing lives, creating community* (5th ed.). Story Center & Routledge. https://doi.org/10.4324/9781351266369

8 Video Editing and Multimodal Composing

You and your MLs are now ready to situate all the components for the digital stories into video editing software. This is the most intense and exciting part of digital storytelling. MLs will likely be excited to see their story come together, but they may also be nervous about the digital skills they will need for this step, especially if learning a new software application. In this chapter, we provide guidance and suggestions that will help you as you work to support your MLs through this stage of the digital storytelling process.

The most important piece of advice we have at the beginning of this stage is to make sure you go through the full digital story creation process in the video editing software you choose before introducing it to your MLs. This will give you a "heads up" about what challenges MLs may face using the software, limitations of the software, and tricky elements that might need some additional instruction. As you work with the software, before introducing it to your MLs, we recommend you create guidance sheets or tutorial videos that will help students through those tough spots (see Figure 4.1 in Chapter 4 for an example).

Our second piece of advice is to now look closely at your results on the technology survey we described in Chapter 4 in order to identify early in the process which MLs have more technological expertise and which have less. If you have not yet given the survey, you may want to modify it based on the software application you have chosen. If you have given the survey already, the results, and specifically knowing what video software MLs might already be familiar with and their prior experience with video editing (if any), can help you decide which video editing software to choose. Using video editing software your MLs are already familiar with might not be an option due to a lack of necessary features for digital storytelling, the inability to install it on school computers, or another reason. However, knowing which MLs have video editing experience will help you identify "technology experts" in the classroom. They can help other MLs with different sorts of video editing questions and tasks, even if they are not as familiar with the software you are using. In addition, based on your MLs' technological strengths and weaknesses, you can group them for support as they work with their digital stories in the video editing software. This

DOI: 10.4324/9781003295730-10

type of collaboration is important as it builds on MLs' strengths and interests, empowers them, and creates a productive and collaborative environment. In Chapter 9, we dive more deeply into the idea of creating a community of practice in your classroom where MLs' various strengths are highlighted to support others' limitations. While no one ML (or teacher!) can be good at everything, a community of practice can support and increase everyone's abilities.

Choosing Video Editing Software

You have probably already been thinking about which video editing software you want to use for digital storytelling with your MLs. In Table 8.1, we indicate basic information and pros and cons for five common applications. As technology is always changing, you will want to verify any information we give here before making a final decision.

Moving from Storyboarding to Video Editing

At this point in the digital storytelling production process, MLs have their storyboards completed and have all media files—voiceover, visuals, and music—organized in folders. No matter which video editing software application you have chosen, MLs will need to get all digital storytelling elements into that application. Some software applications make this quite seamless, such as PowerDirector, which can import folders directly from Google Drive. For others, it is not as easy or intuitive, and folders or individual media elements will need to be imported one-by-one into the application working space. If the video editing software allows it, as iMovie and Final Cut Pro do, it is better to import complete folders. In Chapter 7, we strongly recommend careful organization of folders and components for this reason. Consider demonstrating to your MLs how to import folders or elements, noting that the order they are imported into the software does not matter. However, you will want to ensure at this point that MLs have all elements imported before moving onto the next step.

The next step is for MLs to start working with the video editing timeline to build their digital stories. At this point, the order of components situated into the timeline matters. We recommend MLs place the voiceover onto the timeline first as it determines the length of the digital story. The next step is to place the images and add transitions. Working with the images and transitions and syncing them to the voiceover can take a significant amount of time. Because of the intricate nature of this video editing, we recommend placing the music onto the timeline as the last step. If you have MLs who want to hear their music with the voiceover and images from the beginning, you might encourage them to remove the music from the timeline while editing and then place it back in to check their work,

Table 8.1 Video editing software options chart

Name	*Availability/cost*	*Overview*	*Pros*	*Cons*	*Notes*
iMovie https://www.apple.com/imovie/	This software is included with or can be downloaded free of charge to all Apple products (i.e., MacBook laptop, iPad, iPhone, etc.).	This is high-quality video editing software with a variety of video editing features. It is rather easy to use and navigate and has many online tutorials available.	• MLs tend to have experience with this app. • It can be used without Internet connection. • You can edit your digital story across different devices by air dropping them.	• This software can be overwhelming to users with lower technological literacy skills due to the variety of video editing features and the number of choices. • It is only available on Apple products.	Heather uses this successfully with university students and recommends using it with middle and high schoolers as well. Many of Polina's university students choose this for their digital storytelling projects.
Final Cut Pro https://www.apple.com/final-cut-pro/	You can try this software out with a free trial for 90 days. To purchase, it is a one-time charge of $299.99.	This is the video editing tool that professionals use, with all the features needed for high-quality video editing.	• This is the most powerful editing tool available. • There is an abundance of video editing features.	• This software can only be used on Apple laptops, desktops, or iPads. • This software cannot be used on hand-held devices or PCs. • This software will likely be overwhelming for novice users due to high number of video editing features and tools.	Heather and Polina both trained on this software and use it for their personal stories. Both, however, find other free or less expensive tools just as good for working with MLs.

(*Continued*)

Table 8.1 (Continued)

Name	*Availability/cost*	*Overview*	*Pros*	*Cons*	*Notes*
ClipChamp https://clipchamp.com/en/	This software is freely available online or downloaded. It comes pre-installed on Windows 11 devices. It is a Microsoft product but can be used on any computer. You can have more features by paying $12.00 per month or $120.00 for a year.	This newer video editing app replaces Windows MovieMaker. It is easy to use with many features not usually found in free software, including unlimited video creation.	The numerous advantages of this software include: • Unlimited exporting of videos you create, • Free stock elements and effects, • Auto-captioning in 140 languages, • Unique tools like a "speaker coach" to improve voiceover quality, • Templates and AI to support fast video creation, and • In-app explanation of effect options.	• If you use advanced features within the free plan, the final product will have a watermark. • There are significantly more music options than stock images with the free plan. • There are limited options for transitions between images with the free plan.	Heather and Polina have not yet used this software, but the options available with the free version make it an attractive choice. It is important to choose this only if you are in a teaching context with reliable internet access or where the desktop app can be downloaded.
WeVideo https://www.wevideo.com	This software has a free version, with limited features, production, and storage, but you have to create an account. For the unlimited plan, the cost is $8.00 to $16.00 per month. Special teacher pricing is available for $25.00 per month for up to 30 MLs.	This is a newer, popular application for video editing which includes easy-to-use templates, making the video production process faster. Even the free version offers high-quality options but is limited to only five minutes of video exporting per month.	• This app is easy to use and popular, meaning MLs might have experience using it. • It offers basic and more advanced editor options for mixed-ability classes. • There is an overview tutorial in the app. • It contains multiple stock images and music that can be used to experiment or to demonstrate to MLs.	• You must have online access to use this app. • The free version has a watermark when publishing the final product. • The title slides and other effects are limited in the free version, but all options can be seen. It will be important to instruct MLs which they can use.	This is the video editing software Polina and Heather plan to use for their next project. The free version is limited, but they feel it will be good enough for shorter and simpler projects.

PowerDirector https://www.cyberlink.com/	This software is freely available to download for Mac (Apple products) or PCs. It can also be downloaded as an app on Chromebooks, iPads or other tablets, and any smartphone. When opening, you can choose the free version or PowerDirector 365 for about $70.00 per year or about $20.00 per month.	This software is very easy to navigate with an intuitive user interface, especially for MLs who have lower literacy or technological literacy levels. The free version includes a variety of video editing features including transitions, special effects, and music.	• This software can be seamlessly integrated with Google Drive. • It contains stock images, videos, and music that can be used to experiment or demonstrate to MLs. • MLs can record their voiceovers directly into the app.	• The final products have a large watermark if using the free version. • The additional transitions, title slides, and other effects in the pay version are visible in the free version, but not accessible.	Polina used this software successfully with adults with lower literacy levels on Chromebooks (see featured digital storytelling project in Chapter 5). Polina and Heather also used this software with the "We Live in La Crosse: Stories of Belonging" project (see featured digital storytelling project in Chapter 11) on Mac desktops.

until they are happy with their digital story. Here we provide detailed information for each element in the order we recommend they be added to the timeline.

Voiceover

The first step in building a digital story in the timeline of video editing software is dragging and dropping the audio recording of the verbal narrative—the voiceover—onto an audio line. In most video editing applications, you can use the mouse to drag an audio file with the voiceover onto the timeline. Note that as you drop it, the software will put the voiceover onto the appropriate audio line. Once MLs position their voiceover on the timeline, make sure to instruct them to leave some space on the timeline at the beginning before the voiceover starts. This will be the space for the title slide. Some digital stories have a bit of background music or even silence before the voiceover begins, often for about five seconds. If the voiceover starts by stating the title of the digital story and the name of the author, extra space at the beginning might not be necessary and will be easy to eliminate later. We suggest alerting MLs to think about these nuances before they place their voiceover on the timeline. If your MLs have two or more voiceover clips, this is the time they will place them sequentially onto the timeline.

Visuals—Images and Video Clips

Once the voiceover is placed on the timeline and aligned the way they want, MLs can start placing their visual components on the timeline. First, have MLs create a blank title slide and insert it as a placeholder before placing their first image in the timeline. It is a good idea at this point to tell MLs they will also be adding credit slides at the end of the timeline, but these can be added later without the need to put in placeholders now. Most video editing software allows creators to drag and drop images and video clips onto the timeline; images and video clips will automatically go on separate lines. In addition, most software has a default amount of time each image will appear on the screen (usually three to five seconds).

As MLs first place their images, we suggest they do so without thinking about transitions, alignment with the voiceover, special effects, or any other fine-tuning yet. The first step is to just focus on sequencing the images. We suggest dropping the visuals in the order MLs have them on their storyboards. It can be useful to have MLs' storyboards printed out so they can see that order and avoid switching screens between their storyboards and video editing software on their computers, making the process easier and faster.

After visuals are sequenced in the order that MLs originally envisioned in their storyboards, they can play their digital story as a draft in the video viewing window in the software. They can also begin to see how they need to align images with the voiceover and whether they have enough visuals for the amount of time of their voiceover or if they have too few or too many. In our experience, MLs very often at this point realize that they need more images or need to repeat some of the images they have to complete their multimodal messages. MLs might also decide they are not happy with a particular image and want to swap it with another that has been already uploaded into the software or not. In either case, it is easy enough to swap out an image. However, going through this process, MLs will have to make some difficult decisions about what images to keep or remove. Peer editing and collaboration can be helpful here to give MLs the audience's perspective. MLs might also realize that they need to split their verbal narrative in chunks to accommodate video clips where the sound carries its own meaning and contributes to the overall narration in their digital stories. Alternatively, they might need to eliminate the sound in video clips so it does not interfere with their verbal narration. This fine-tuning between the verbal narrative and visuals of a digital story requires multimodal decision making, patience, and careful manipulation of the media on their timeline. Luckily, every video editing software has an undo button, so the students can experiment and undo their actions to get back to the previous editing stage.

After images and video clips are lined up with the verbal narrative and in the desired sequence, MLs can work on the amount of time each image is on screen, transitions, and special effects. MLs will need to manipulate the visuals, making still images show on the screen a shorter or longer amount of time and determining if their video clips (if they are using any) need to be edited (for example, cut shorter or split). For example, MLs might want to keep some images on the screen longer than others if one image lines up with a longer section of the voiceover or to indicate reflection or resolution. Alternatively, images can be shown in more rapid succession (only one or two seconds on screen), to indicate movement or change in the narrative. Most video editing software applications come with several options for transitions. It can be helpful to demonstrate to MLs some of the most common (cross-dissolve, Ken Burns, etc.) to give them a place to start. You might also want to view a digital story or two again to have MLs notice and analyze the transitions. It is important to have MLs consider how transitions are used in multimodal composing and contribute to the telling of the narrative. For example, the Ken Burns effect can be used to zoom into a particular area on an image, focusing the audience on a particular part of the narrative.

It is possible that transitions and special effects will shift the length of visuals, requiring MLs to adjust and work on their visual components on the timeline again. This fine-tuning can take time and again requires patience. When time is limited or MLs have lower levels of technological literacy, it might be advisable to use only still images and not look for sophisticated video effects. This will make the video editing process simpler and more straightforward. In our experience working with middle schoolers, university students, and adults, MLs themselves usually make these decisions based on their comfort levels with technology. Every once in a while we have had MLs who knew significantly more about video editing than we did and were eager to work on their own and apply various video editing techniques. For example, the author of the digital story *My Big Foot* (https://youtu.be/Jcsk2R8_esM; produced in Heather's class in fall 2008) was a media studies major well versed in video production. She produced her digital story on her own without seeking help with video editing. MLs usually work at their comfort level, and we have seen again and again that digital stories without special effects and with only some basic transitions are able to transmit powerful multimodal messages.

Background Music

MLs can add their background music once the timeline with the voiceover and visuals is finalized. The first step is to have MLs drag and drop their background music onto the timeline. Typically, although not always, music starts at the beginning of a digital story and continues through the credits. Have MLs notice if their music is long enough. If the music file is shorter than the verbal narrative, they will need to look for a creative solution to address it. For example, they can use the same music file, dropping it again after the first one ends. They can also cut and paste different sections of the music file. Another solution is to shift the music so it starts later in the digital story and ends earlier, before the final credits. Whichever option is chosen, MLs should keep in mind their multimodal composition and how the meaning of their story is conveyed with the music. It is not necessary to worry about volume now, but MLs may want to go ahead and lower the volume across the board on the background music so they can more easily hear their voiceover as they do more fine-tuning of their digital story.

> Watch the digital story *Me and Military*; https://youtu.be/MZkzO-pneXA. Note where and how the music begins and where it ends. What other multimodal means does the author use to make the start of the music meaningful? This digital story was produced in Polina's class in summer 2008.

Now that each of the digital story elements are in place in the timeline, MLs will want to again think about multimodal composing and multimodal messages of their digital story. They may notice that their images and voiceover are repetitive in certain areas and decide to either eliminate an image or cut a section of the voiceover. They may want to find another piece of music to create a different mood or highlight a particular section of their narrative. As MLs watch and rewatch their story, they will start fine-tuning their digital story. We next describe this intense video editing process that will shape the digital story into a true multimodal masterpiece.

Fine-tuning the Digital Story

For each element of the digital story, there are additional options that MLs can explore. We present the information in the following order, but it is likely that most MLs will move back and forth between elements, as editing one element impacts the others.

Voiceover

At any stage of the video editing process, MLs may decide that their voiceover does not work as well as they had thought. They may not be happy with the sound quality, the speed, or their voice for various reasons. They may want to re-record. We suggest first identifying the issue and seeing if re-recording is really necessary. If the issue is lining up the voiceover to images, MLs can edit their voiceover to better align with images by adding or deleting pauses. If MLs are sure they want to re-record and the issue is alignment, have MLs watch their images as they record. Other reasons to consider re-recording are missing words or parts of the verbal narrative, too many verbal fillers such as "um" that are distracting to the listener, or other issues with comprehensibility. No matter the issue, it is best to re-record early, and before going any further in the video editing process.

Once MLs are happy with the voiceover and it is aligned to images, it is time to adjust the volume. While this process happens in tandem with the background music, there may be some need to increase or decrease the volume at certain points in the voiceover. If there are two or more voiceover segments, matching the volume of each is important. MLs can use fade-out and fade-in on the volume control to make the transition between voiceover segments more seamless.

Text on Screen and Subtitles

It is now time for MLs to decide if they want to add text on screen and/or subtitles. We differentiate text on screen from subtitles as they serve different multimodal purposes. Subtitles are likely to be added throughout the entire digital story if MLs want to use them, but they can also be added strategically at certain points. To add subtitles, a completed digital story can be uploaded to YouTube where subtitles can be easily added automatically.

MLs can edit the captions that are automatically generated, even deleting subtitles where they are not necessary or MLs do not want them. If uploading to YouTube is not possible or desirable, MLs can add text slides with subtitles on them wherever they feel it is necessary. Text slides are usually blank slides that go on one of the video lines of the timeline and can be overlaid with the other media elements without disrupting or breaking them apart. There will be some fine-tuning necessary to ensure subtitles align with the voiceover, images, and transitions.

Text on screen is a kind of special effect added to visuals that can be used to engage in translanguaging, emphasize a point, and add another layer of multimodal meaning. MLs can choose to strategically position text on screen, from a single word to a phrase or a complete sentence in any language of their choice. To do so, they will need to use text slides and overlay them with visuals or insert them between the visuals. Inserting text slides between the visuals will make their visual timeline longer, so it is advisable to make these decisions at an earlier stage, while building and fine-tuning the visual timeline.

> Watch again the digital story *A Good (Hmong) Woman*; https://youtu.be/aOGYcDhxPgs. Note how the creator used text on screen, as well as images, to convey her translingual message. This digital story was produced in Heather's class in spring 2022.

Visuals

Now that the images are in place, MLs may want to consider adding other special effects to their images. In our experience, MLs will find and add in special effects on their own depending on their knowledge of technology and desire to create another layer of meaning. We do not usually include any additional or special instructions on special effects as it can be unnecessarily overwhelming for MLs with lower levels of technological literacy. Depending on the MLs you have, it might be worthwhile mentioning this step to them, but leaving it as optional.

Generally speaking, we recommend the option of using videos in digital stories for those MLs who are more experienced in the process. However, videos are becoming easier and easier to edit and use every year, so you may want to allow your MLs to add this medium. This might be a good time for MLs curious about video production to experiment and play with video editing as they are in the safe space of your class. But they need to be aware that video editing might take longer than working only with still images so that they, and you, can allocate time accordingly.

> Watch again the digital story *From Guatemala to the US*; https://www.youtube.com/watch?v=lcYjs35fcKo&t=296s. Note how the creator integrated videos in her project that she produced using PowerDirector. It was this adult migrant's first time working on a digital story and using video editing software. This digital story was produced in Carlye Steven's class in summer 2022.

Music

The considerations with background music are similar to those of the voiceover, with volume being the first. Background music is typically louder when there is silence in the voiceover, and then quieter when the voiceover comes in. In cases where music with lyrics is used, MLs might choose to use the message of the lyrics as a part of the narrative, making it louder and more highlighted at those points. MLs can also choose to use more than one song in their digital story, or a compilation of tunes that reflect different moods and differently accentuate their narrative. Fading the music in and out can make those transitions smoother and less noticeable. If the music is not long enough for the digital story, MLs may choose a particular part of the song to copy and add to the end. This clipping is also managed best with fading in and out effects.

Finalizing the Digital Story

Once MLs have built their timelines, situated all their multimodal components, checked their timelines in the movie viewing window several times, and are satisfied with the result of their video editing work, they are ready to export their digital stories into the movie format. This necessary step will allow them to have a movie file they will be able to save and play independently of the video editing software.

This process of exporting involves a few decisions as well, depending on the software application you use. Most have the option to export a higher quality video, but this requires more time to complete and greater memory capacity to store. Lower quality videos take less time to export but the quality of the final product may or may not be noticeably affected. You may want to experiment with your own digital story first to see what your hardware can handle, in terms of storage, how long it takes to export at various quality levels, and if the final product is noticeably different depending on export level. Note that if after exporting you decide to upload your or your MLs' digital story files online, for example to YouTube, you will also be able to decrease the quality level then, keeping the highest possible quality level of the digital story file on your device.

After exporting, it is crucial to check the volume of the voiceover and the music. We have found that the volume of one or the other often has to be adjusted when exporting to ensure that both can be heard but that one does not overpower the other. You should plan enough time for MLs to export their digital stories at least twice to take care of any volume or other issues that may arise. At the end of this process, MLs should have a digital story that they are proud of and excited to share with each other.

You may have some MLs who are hesitant to finalize their digital story and export it. They may be tweaking and modifying in very minor ways, having a hard time being satisfied with their final product. It is a good idea to talk to MLs about knowing when a digital story is good enough. We are not professional video producers! We could edit for a very long time, but for most of our purposes, digital stories that are not perfect are just fine.

In the featured digital storytelling project below, we see a teacher using Flipgrid (https://info.flip.com/) to have MLs engage in digital multimodal composing on the topic of social justice. While the project does not ask MLs to tell personal stories, as is more typical in digital storytelling, MLs give personal opinions about social justice topics that are important to them. Depending on the goals, class time, and available technology, this can be a useful format in a multilingual class and can follow the steps and approaches of digital storytelling production that we focus on in this book.

In Chapter 10, we focus on sharing digital stories in your classroom and beyond and discuss how valuable that part of the process is. Meanwhile, in the next chapter, Chapter 9, we revisit how student collaboration takes place throughout the digital storytelling process and why it is valuable. Specifically, we explore some of the ways that peer editing can be useful throughout the digital storytelling process, discuss how translanguaging can be integrated in this collaborative work, and talk more about creating a strong and supportive community of practice with your MLs.

Featured digital storytelling project: Social issues—I am concerned about …

Name: Nada Filipovic
Position: English Language Teacher and Teaching Advisor, Sabacka gimnazija grammar school
Project Name and Location: Sabac, Serbia

Being an EFL teacher for years in a country that has been struggling with poverty, serious ecological issues, emigration, and brain drain, I decided to create a digital storytelling project where some of the issues would be dealt with and, moreover, the voices of my students would be heard. Traditionally, we have been raised to be humble and not to express our views on matters that influence our lives. For that reason, too, I wanted to encourage my students to express their feelings and share their opinion on the things that matter and that will help us live in a more democratic society.

I started the project in my classes with 10th graders (students aged 16 to 17) in the late winter of 2022. The goal was to have the students do some research on social issues in Serbia and choose the most important ones that needed an urgent reaction. In classes, I encouraged them to discuss their ideas first, within groups of four—the groups were formed in accordance with the issues they were addressing (e.g., one group dealt with corruption and similar problems). The goal was to raise awareness of these issues and highlight the importance of expressing their concerns as a sort of call to action.

Most of the reliable sources on the topic were in their mother tongue so my students had to use translanguaging in order to make these videos in English. Individually, they recorded short videos on the topic on Flipgrid platform. The platform is easy to use and even the free version has lots of video effects, sounds, and visuals that can be added to make stories more vivid and interesting. Moreover, students can like or leave comments to one another's videos, which makes the stories go further in this "virtual grid." The students were curious not only to tell the stories but to explore these features in order to make the audience focused and involved. To my amazement, even shyer students who were hesitant to talk in front of others liked the educational tool very much. It is important to note that automated subtitles in English are another feature of Flipgrid.

Having recorded their digital stories, the students felt their ideas should be heard by more people. It was they who suggested sharing these videos with the Students' Parliament in our school. The Students' Parliament organized a meeting where we all together watched the stories. Students in the school and in the local community and NGOs are very good in English. Therefore, at the meeting the students talked solely in English. Interestingly, some of the Parliament members shared their ideas on social issues immediately. That was the moment I saw the digital world and our own just merged and that stories in all forms easily connect people. The students were satisfied and eager to take action. The next step was to connect to NGOs that could help them do something about things they had been concerned about. Thanks to the Centre of Culture in our hometown, which gladly invited us to their premises, the cooperation with the NGOs began. When we presented, some comments on the stories were in Serbian by those who felt less adept or confident in English. Since then, local NGOs have already launched some projects on human rights and gender equity (in which lots of my students have been participating).

When I realized how eager and enthusiastic my students were, I decided to share this activity with my fellow colleagues in ELTA (the national English Language Teachers' Association). I gave a workshop where I presented my students' work. My colleagues were touched and sympathetic—they found our students were the wind of change we had desperately needed and that we had to motivate them to tell the stories they considered important. Hopefully a number of teachers have started this activity and they use the platform for digital stories on various topics.

Everybody has their story to tell, all we need is to encourage them and give them some time and room of their own. Literally and metaphorically, using Flipgrid we have created story circulation. We are all made of stories and we all have some story to tell.

The project is available at https://flip.com/985df492 but first a person needs to sign up to Flipgrid and then click on the link. It's free.

9 Peer Collaboration and Feedback

We have shown in previous chapters how peer feedback and collaboration can be used with each stage of the digital storytelling process. We also noted that having MLs working together in meaningful ways can be motivating to their learning (see Chapter 5). In this chapter, we focus more deeply on theories of collaboration and how collaboration is especially useful and productive for digital storytelling projects. We also hone in on how collaboration in the digital storytelling process can be multilingual, harnessing the full potential of translanguaging for MLs. We include multiple activities and resources that we have used that will hopefully help you through this process. Let's go!

Communities of Practice

One of the foundational understandings of digital storytelling is that it is a collaborative process. By working with others, we can create digital stories that are more powerful and more engaging. *Communities of practice*, or CoP (Wenger, 1998), is a theory that explains the importance of collaboration. The theory of CoP challenges the idea that learning is an individual process, or separate from what we do in the rest of our lives. Rather, Wenger (1998) asks us to assume that "learning is, in its essence, a fundamentally social phenomenon, reflecting our own deeply social nature as human beings capable of knowing" (p. 3). Learning involves more than constructing knowledge or becoming competent in a certain area or task, such as language learning or digital multimodal composing. It also involves identifying with the social community in which we participate and are learning. Meaning, practice, community, and identity are all important in the process of learning. As Wenger explains, the learning process should include "inventive ways of engaging students in meaningful practices, or providing access to resources that enhance their participation, of opening their horizons so they can put themselves on learning trajectories they can identify with, and of involving them in actions, discussions, and reflections that

DOI: 10.4324/9781003295730-11

make a difference to the communities they value" (p. 10). For these reasons, we believe that the theory of CoP explains very well the collaborative nature of digital storytelling and digital storytelling projects.

We all have multiple CoP to which we belong, including our family, our work, our hobbies, or volunteer groups, among others, and our membership in these CoP is different. We may be core members in a few CoP and more peripheral members in others. Learning, according to Lave and Wenger (1991), is like becoming a member of a CoP. They call this process *legitimate peripheral participation*, drawing parallels with various trades (electricians, plumbers, etc.) that have strong apprenticeship learning programs. They argue that a new member in any CoP changes their participation and transforms their identity in the CoP over time. We might think of the identity transformation that takes place when someone becomes an advanced speaker of their second language (see Norton [2001] for more on this topic). Indeed, English speakers worldwide could be considered a CoP in which millions identify and participate every day as they learn more.

What does this mean for our digital storytelling projects? Teachers have become increasingly aware of the importance of creating a positive classroom and school community in which our MLs identify as a part of the community and can learn to the best of their ability. In our classrooms, we want to create a collaborative and supportive CoP that facilitates productive language learning and positive perspectives on multilingual identities. We also want to introduce the CoP of digital storytellers to our MLs. Some of our MLs will already be experts and members of this CoP if they are creating videos on YouTube and/or digital content on TikTok or other social media platforms. Others will be novices and engage in legitimate peripheral participation as they learn from experts in the classroom. Teachers can be among the experts in the classroom or, in some areas of DS work, they may be novices. Your own engagement in the CoP will change over time as you learn more and become more involved in digital storytelling and digital multimodal composing as a part of the digital storytelling process. We encourage you to engage with StoryCenter and other online digital storytelling groups to develop a more core identity as a digital storyteller, and thus learn more.

The collaborative approach to digital storytelling allows your MLs to enter the CoP where they are. They are legitimate members of the CoP, whether they are experts able to fully participate or they are learning as legitimate peripheral participants. The philosophy of CoP recognizes that we are all learning all the time from, and with, each other. There are no benefits of membership that are held back until an ML is a "real" digital storyteller or knows everything about digital storytelling. Rather, anyone can enter this CoP at any time and identify as a digital storyteller from the beginning. It is the most democratizing of learning possible.

CoP in action in your classroom means encouraging and engaging learners in collaboration at all stages of the digital storytelling process. This looks like:

1. Recognizing your own digital storytelling strengths and limitations, and those of your MLs;
2. Highlighting technological skills and abilities needed in the CoP and providing resources (including the MLs themselves) that can help as they are practiced and learned;
3. Purposefully creating groups of MLs who are more or less peripheral and core in their membership in the digital storytelling CoP;
4. Expecting all members of the CoP to mentor and support all others as members of the CoP;
5. Respecting and valuing where each ML is as a member of the CoP, and that some students may want to only be peripheral members while others become core members; and
6. Recognizing your own membership as more or less core in the CoP.

Finally, a key piece of CoPs in our classroom digital storytelling projects is shifting the view of collaboration. Instead of seeing individual work as the ideal and rejecting collaboration as cheating or somehow not doing one's best, the digital storytelling CoP emphasizes collaborative learning from and with each other. Here are examples of how participants (all names are pseudonyms) in the "We Live in La Crosse" summer digital storytelling workshop engaged in and benefited from the CoP approach.

Wanda

Wanda was an adult Mandarin Chinese speaker who migrated from China to the United States. She came to the workshop as a highly proficient English speaker who had never created a digital story or any other digital content. As she became a legitimate peripheral participant in the digital storytelling CoP, she sought out support and help from teenage members to digitally compose her story. She was a core member of the English-speaker CoP, very comfortable in that role, but her lack of experience in the digital storytelling CoP meant she collaborated with others to learn.

Vanessa

Vanessa was a young multilingual Spanish speaker, born in the United States. She was also a core member of the English-speaker CoP and she had more digital multimodal composing experience than some others. She was a legitimate peripheral participant in storytelling and used examples of other MLs' narrative writing to help her craft her own in a more narrative style.

Jessica

Jessica was a young recent immigrant from the Philippines and was a legitimate peripheral participant in the English-speaker CoP. She was highly engaged in digital content (podcasts, videos, social media), yet also was a legitimate peripheral participant in the digital storytelling CoP as she had not created her own yet. She was supported by several others in the workshop as she learned language and digital storytelling skills.

These examples demonstrate how MLs can participate in their various CoPs at different levels. In the English-speaking CoP, some are core participants for whom English is the main linguistic medium of communication. Others take on more peripheral roles as they are learning to communicate in English in various settings and for various purposes. In our examples, some participants are already members of the CoP that engages in digital multimodal composing of various types while others are complete novices. As all of our workshop participants were engaging in digital storytelling work, they were collaborating, learning from each other, and creating a classroom CoP that further facilitated development of their digital literacy skills and, for some, their language skills. In this way, digital stories and activities that accompany their production have great potential to facilitate a CoP in a language class.

Preparing learners for collaboration and peer feedback

Not all MLs have experience collaborating in school or being asked to give peer feedback. It is important to model and provide MLs with reasons why collaboration and peer feedback are so helpful. We hope that the activities and worksheets we offer in this book will give you ideas on how to prepare MLs for and engage in various collaborative tasks. We also recommend identifying peer leaders in a class—MLs who have leadership skills, are respected by their classmates, demonstrate eagerness to help, or have more advanced digital literacy skills—to be group facilitators, leads on some activities, or helpers during digital storytelling work.

Translanguaging Communities of Practice and Collaboration in Digital Storytelling

In our classrooms, we want to create a multilingual CoP where learners' various languages, backgrounds, and life stories are welcomed and integrated into the learning process. Translanguaging can be a useful pedagogical approach that creates space for multiple languages in a productive and systematic way. We discussed translanguaging extensively in Chapter

3. In this chapter, we want to reiterate that while translanguaging supports home languages in an English language classroom, it also recognizes and builds on varying degrees of MLs' English language proficiency, thus taking on an asset-based perspective rather than a deficiency mindset. As Marrero-Colón (2021) emphasizes, translanguaging "allows the integration and collaboration of language learners from all proficiency levels" (p. 8). As our MLs are more or less skilled speakers of English, translanguaging can help them move from peripheral to core membership in the classroom CoP. We also suggest that translanguaging can facilitate its own CoP. Some MLs may be core members, already engaging in translanguaging and demonstrating pride in their multilingual repertoire. Other MLs may be legitimate peripheral participants in this CoP, having or being surrounded by a monolingual mindset. Through collaboration, MLs can move from legitimate peripheral participation to becoming core members of the translanguaging CoP.

In our work, we have seen MLs translanguage when they needed to reach out to their families and friends for help with visuals or music, when brainstorming and discussing their ideas for digital stories, and when seeking peer help and feedback from others who share the same languages (Vinogradova, 2011). Yet, MLs are often surprised that we want them to use other languages in their digital stories. Translingual practices might not come as easily to MLs as we might expect, and some MLs do not recognize ways they can translanguage in their digital stories. Even when reporting conversations between family members or addressing their parents, MLs can be hesitant to incorporate their home languages in their multimodal narratives. They might not see a legitimate place for their home languages in an English language class and, as discussed previously in Chapter 7, MLs can worry that the teacher and other classmates won't fully understand their stories. Nevertheless, we, like others (see Castañeda et al., 2018; Jiang et al., 2020), have found that incorporating home languages in digital storytelling projects increases MLs' engagement in the target language (Vinogradova et al., 2011).

Translanguaging in digital stories especially legitimizes and empowers the multilingual language practices of MLs who come from minoritized language backgrounds in their home countries. These multilingual practices become acts of advocacy and empowerment for MLs who are often mislabeled as native speakers of dominant languages in their countries of origin (Pentón Herrera, 2019). In the next section, we provide suggestions for ways to incorporate the CoP approach with digital storytelling projects. We also discuss ways to scaffold and facilitate translanguaging with MLs while they are going through the steps of digital story production. This scaffolding will create space for MLs to incorporate their home languages and legitimize this language use as part of multimodal practices.

Getting Started

It is important that an approach including collaboration and the theory of CoP be initiated from the beginning of the digital storytelling process. If this is not your typical classroom practice, MLs need to see and experience from the beginning the collaboration that is expected in this project. We suggested in Chapter 4 that you determine your MLs' language and technological abilities before beginning a digital storytelling project. Typically, as educators, we are trying to teach our lessons at the midrange of MLs' abilities, knowing that we will have to differentiate to support MLs at the lower range of language proficiency and challenge those at the higher range in our classes. With this project, while conscious of our MLs' abilities, we also want to recognize that collaboration and the learning that happens through social interaction can stretch MLs' abilities beyond what they can do by themselves. What may be new for some teachers in this process is that the MLs themselves support each other as they collaborate and learn.

At the beginning stage, as MLs view several examples of digital stories, collaboration can help them analyze how language is used in the stories. You may group MLs by language background so they can translanguage as they notice the choices made by digital story creators as they use one or multiple languages. In collaborative groups, MLs can answer prompts such as:

- What language(s) are used in this story?
- At what points does the creator transition between languages? Why do you think the creator does that?
- How does the creator support (or not) understanding for those who do not speak one or more of the languages used in the story?
- What do you think about the choices the creator made regarding language in the story?

Brainstorming

Collaboration and translanguaging naturally support MLs at the point of generating ideas for their digital stories. Here are three possible collaborative activities that take advantage of MLs' different languages and readiness for narrative storytelling.

1. Especially for groups of MLs who are younger or at lower language or literacy levels, it can be very helpful to provide some possible story ideas, such as family, cultural practices, favorite things to do, immigration stories, or language learning stories. You can designate different areas of the classroom as different spaces to discuss these possible topics (for example, by placing a sign in each corner with one possible topic on it) and then have groups of MLs discuss for five to ten minutes and then rotate

through each area. MLs with similar language backgrounds can be in groups together to encourage translanguaging as they generate ideas. When suggesting story ideas we recommend keeping them open and broad to create room for personal choice and creativity.

2. For more advanced MLs in terms of language proficiency, literacy levels, or age, you can provide prompts and time for individual reflection and pair or group discussion. For example, you can give the prompt, "What aspect of your life would you like to share?" and ask MLs to free write about the topic for five minutes. The free write can be in English or any other language. Then, MLs can be paired to discuss their ideas in whatever language makes the most sense to them.
3. For groups of MLs who are more resistant to the idea of telling their own story, consider using this process that makes the brainstorming fully collaborative. Organize groups of four to five MLs and provide each one with a story starter. A few examples are, "Something good that has happened in our classroom is …" or "Something we like about where we live is …." Then, the first ML in the group finishes the sentence and passes it to the next ML. That ML has to write the next sentence, and the paper gets passed around, with each ML adding a sentence. The sentences can be added in any language, with drawings or translations used to support understanding. When finished, the MLs can use any portion of any of the ideas generated.

In these ways, the brainstorming process sets MLs up to be collaborative, encourages thinking about topics and themes interesting to them, helps them see how other MLs are engaging in the narrative process, and prepares them for translanguaging throughout the entire digital storytelling process.

Story Circle

The story circle is by definition a collaborative space, and it can easily be a translanguaging space as well. When MLs are presenting their story ideas they can use their full linguistic repertoire, as can those listening and offering feedback. Even if the story circle is mostly in English, due to the linguistic make-up of the class or MLs' preferences, as MLs talk about their ideas for their digital stories they can describe how their brainstorming process utilized translanguaging (such as when taking notes, recording thoughts, talking to different people, etc.) and helped them get to this point with their story. In this way, MLs see clear examples of how translanguaging is useful and an expected tool to support academic work. During the story circle, you may also guide MLs to think about (or question each other about) how their language(s) might be presented in their digital stories in various modalities (e.g., virtually, through music). The mock story circle we suggested in Chapter 6, where you present your digital story idea to MLs and demonstrate to them how they can ask questions, can be especially helpful to model the translanguaging aspect of the story circle.

Verbal Narrative

As MLs write their verbal narrative, collaboration is an option that can be helpful, especially for MLs who are less confident in English and/or writing narratives. Rather than waiting to do peer feedback after a draft is written, as we suggest in Chapter 6, here we provide a few ideas for collaboration and peer support earlier in the writing process.

- MLs in English-speaking environments (such as in the US) tend to have stronger speaking skills than writing skills as they communicate orally in English every day. We suggest harnessing the oral language strengths of MLs as they work on their written narratives by pairing two MLs to work together. One will explain their story idea orally as the other (potentially more advanced in writing skills) completes a graphic organizer with the main ideas. Then, the original ML can use the completed graphic organizer to develop their narrative.
- Young MLs may not have much experience writing narratives and might feel more comfortable drawing ideas for their stories. If you start with drawings, MLs can then be paired to explain their drawing and story to each other and can be encouraged to do so using their full linguistic repertoire. Finally, in pairs, MLs work to move from the oral story to a written narrative, supporting each other.
- For MLs who are struggling to move their narrative forward on paper, you may want to return to the third suggestion under *Brainstorming* given previously. In this case, an ML can provide the opening sentence or idea for their story, and then pass the paper to another person to have them flesh out more details of the story. It is likely in this case that the original ML will have to rework some of the writing, but this editing can be easier than writing from scratch.
- MLs who have lower literacy levels can be encouraged to record their audio narrative directly without the writing step. In this case, the verbally recorded narrative (the voiceover) will undergo several rounds of editing and revision in collaboration with peers and be re-recorded several times. Translanguaging is at the forefront as MLs decide what to record in the various languages, addressing questions of authenticity of voice, language expectations, and audience understanding.

At this point, it is important to address translanguaging explicitly with all your MLs. You can ask thought-provoking questions such as "How could you convey the message to a different audience? Which audience are you addressing here? In what other ways can you support audience understanding, besides the oral narrative?" To encourage and support translanguaging, remind MLs that subtitles or other text on screen can be used at any time to support audience comprehension.

Storyboarding

In Chapter 7, we provided several ideas for peer editing and collaboration in the storyboarding process. Here we offer a worksheet that MLs can use to give feedback to each other on their storyboard. Questions 6, 7, and 8 are helpful as MLs think about and plan where they will use translanguaging in their digital stories, making conscious decisions about what languages they use and at what points in their stories. Peer collaborators from other language backgrounds can be especially useful in determining what is understood, and how, in the digital story. Here we would like to also suggest MLs be given the opportunity, and encouraged, to collaborate with friends and family members to help find visuals, give more details in their stories, or support them in their digital storytelling in other ways. Such collaboration beyond the classroom engages MLs and others more deeply in the digital storytelling process.

Worksheet: Questions for storyboarding peer feedback

1. How does the digital story grab your attention at the beginning?
2. What emotion is conveyed in the digital story?
3. Is there a point of tension and then resolution or a moment of change in the digital story?
4. How do the images support what is stated in the verbal narrative?
5. Are there any images that are extraneous or places where more images are needed?
6. Does your partner use more than one language in their digital story?
7. Does your partner plan to use subtitles or other text on screen when using multiple languages in their digital story? How will this help support audience comprehension?
8. Does the digital story feel like it is finished? What else could be added?
9. How does the music chosen help tell the story and contribute to the emotional aspect of the digital story?

Multimodal Composing

As MLs situate all the elements of their digital stories into the chosen software application, it is time to really start using the CoP to its full advantage. No doubt MLs will have a wide range of abilities and experiences with technology. Having MLs collaborate and support each other as they situate their elements is very helpful and further encourages MLs to learn with and from each other. Consider the following suggestions as MLs go through this step:

1. From the technological survey, identify MLs in your class who have experience with your particular software application or skills you want MLs to learn. Because it may be that your MLs have greater abilities than you, ask MLs in the class to demonstrate how to upload images into the software, insert the voiceover, or how to do another video editing task. Acknowledging their expertise empowers MLs. You can also encourage translanguaging in the demonstrations, further underscoring your commitment to linguistic diversity and language maintenance and learning.
2. Incorporate frequent peer sharing sessions. During these sessions, have MLs share with each other where they are in the digital storytelling process. Focus each session on a particular aspect (i.e., the voiceover) and how it works within the message and construction of the full digital story.
3. Focus specifically on translanguaging choices as MLs edit and finalize their digital stories. Discuss as a whole class or in small groups or pairs decisions related to adding subtitles, the use of language(s) on the title slide and credits, other text on screen, and sound and visual effects.
4. Once MLs are ready with a "final" draft, pair them to peer review, focusing on the overall multimodal cohesion and meaning of the story. See our suggested questions that can be used for this peer review.

Multimodal composing peer feedback questions

1. Is the overall message of the digital story clear?
2. Is the message of the digital story told primarily in the images, verbal narrative, music, or a combination of all three?
3. Is there cohesion among all the elements of the digital story?
4. What element(s) signal the moment of change in the digital story?
5. Are there any points in the digital story where you feel confused?

6. How do subtitles support understanding?
7. Does the digital story seem polished enough for the intended audience? If not, in which areas do you recommend more editing?
   a. Transitions between images
   b. Title slide and/or credits
   c. Volume of the verbal narrative and/or music
   d. Other?

Sharing and Presenting

You are now at the happy stage where MLs get to share their digital stories with each other and see reactions to their digital stories in real time. There can be cheers, tears, applause, laughter, and other body language indicating how the audience is responding. As teachers, we are responsible for managing the sharing of the digital stories in the classroom. This is the culminating activity and a very important part of the CoP. You will likely want to remind your MLs how to be respectful audience members. Everyone is vulnerable when sharing their stories, and respectful responses are important. We give many more ideas and strategies related to sharing digital stories in Chapter 10.

Peer feedback is also a very important part of this final stage. You may want to have a feedback sheet such as the one we suggest, or you can have MLs give oral comments to their classmates. Peer feedback can be for the overall production of the digital stories, how they did as a class, on individual digital stories, or as an individual self-reflection on their own digital storytelling process and product. We provide sample worksheets for both of these options.

Peer feedback on individual digital story

Which digital story are you giving feedback on?
Title: ____________________ Creator: ________________________

1. How well did the digital story grab your attention?
2. How well did you understand the message of the digital story?
3. How did the digital story move you emotionally?
4. How did the images, voiceover, and sound work together to tell the story?
5. What was the best part of the digital story?
6. What suggestions would you offer to make the digital story better?

Feedback on class digital stories

*Please provide the digital story title and creator name when talking about an individual digital story.

1. Which digital story had the best attention grabber? What made it so strong?
2. What were some common messages shared in our digital stories?
3. What languages were used in the digital stories? How did that enhance your experience?
4. Which digital story moved you the most emotionally? Why?
5. How did everyone do with digital multimodal composing? What skills are we still learning?
6. Who used background music very effectively?
7. If you were going to create another digital story, who would you ask for help? In what areas?
8. What was the best part of the digital story?
9. What suggestions would you offer to make the digital story better?

It is also possible that your MLs will want to share their finalized digital stories with their friends outside of class, family members, or other community members. Some may want to share their digital stories on their social media pages. Because each ML is the owner of their own digital story, they have the right to choose how to share it, and we encourage this final collaborative step. However, it is also our responsibility to discuss with MLs concerns about sharing their digital stories, such as audience reception, permanence of media online, copywrite, and others.

In the following featured digital storytelling project, Megan Siczek explains how she encouraged collaboration among MLs in her project with digital literacy narratives (DNLs). This project offers a nice example of how a DNL assignment can scaffold and socialize MLs into their new academic CoP. MLs appreciate the assignment as well as they learn so much about the others in CoP with them.

In this chapter, we have considered peer collaboration and feedback in each stage of the digital storytelling process. In the next chapter, we discuss the last stage of the process—how MLs can present and share their digital stories. We cover considerations of privacy, ownership, and copyright in sharing and we discuss how you can support and prepare MLs so that the sharing of their digital stories is a positive and joyful experience.

Featured digital storytelling project: Telling my own language story: Digital literacy narratives in the EAP classroom

Name: Megan M. Siczek
Position: Associate Professor, English for Academic Purposes (EAP), George Washington University
Project Location: Washington, DC, USA

Multilingual international undergraduate students create multimodal digital literacy narratives (DLNs), a type of digital story focused on their literacy experiences, in my EAP oral academic communication course. The course develops students' capacity for oral academic communication, drawing on themes of global learning and internationalization. For more information about this course, see Siczek (2022), Chapter 1. I position this assignment in the first month of the course, when the focus is on orienting students to the communicative expectations of the US undergraduate curriculum, building community, experimenting with new technologies, and expressing themselves creatively. For this assignment, students are asked to create a five-minute digital literacy narrative that chronicles their personal language journey and how it has intersected with English. These DLNs integrate students' narrative voice with multimedia tools such as images, graphics, videos, music, and audio recordings to tell a cohesive and personal story.

I approach this assignment by ensuring that students understand the genre of a DLN, and we watch and discuss several examples together, with a particular focus on the main evaluative criteria for the assignment: (1) preparation/professionalism; (2) narrative coherence of the story; (3) visual and multimodal appeal; (4) delivery; and (5) time management. After explaining the assignment and reviewing sample DLNs, students meet in groups to reflect on their own experiences and perceptions. They are free to translanguage as they consider questions such as:

- What is your linguistic background?
- What are your earliest memories of the English language?
- What do you remember about how and why you learned English?
- How do you feel about English?
- How have your feelings and experiences evolved over time?
- What images and associations do you have with English?
- How does your experience with English relate to your other cultural and linguistic experiences?

They then discuss and share ideas about artifacts that could be used to add dimensionality to their language stories, followed by planning and creating their own DLN using a technology of their choosing (e.g., iMovie, Audacity, Adobe Creative Cloud). After the assignments are submitted, we watch the DLNs together, and students engage in self and peer evaluations using a Google Form.

This assignment centers students' cultural and linguistic experiences as they are beginning to socialize themselves into a new academic discourse community and enables them to feel closer to their diverse classmates. The creativity and expressiveness embedded in the assignment invite translanguaging and the sharing of memories, feelings, and artifacts that give voice to students' multiple—and sometimes conflicting—language experiences. The genre of a DLN also allows culturally and linguistically diverse students to "compose" a multimodal text without the pressure of meeting monolingual standards for the production of a written text or a formal presentation. In line with the value of translanguaging, students are also welcome to draw on their full linguistic repertoires in conveying their language stories.

In reflections at the end of the semester, this is consistently remarked upon as one of students' favorite assignments because they could choose "how" to express themselves and convey their experiences while at the same time learning so much about one another. From an instructional perspective, this is an easy assignment to manage because students are inspired and motivated; they also create so much of the content themselves and have been able to manage the technology independently. The positive outcomes of this assignment make a strong case for the use of digital storytelling to celebrate linguistic diversity and promote inclusivity within our curricula.

Reference

Siczek, M. (Ed.). (2022). *Pedagogical innovations in oral academic communication*. University of Michigan Press.

References

Castañeda, M. E., Shen, X., & Claros Berlioz, E. M. (2018). This is my story: Latinx learners create digital stories during a summer literacy camp. *TESOL Journal*, *9*(4), 1–14. https://doi.org/10.1002/tesj.378

Jiang, L., Yang, M., & Yu, S. (2020). Chinese ethnic minority students' investment in English learning empowered by digital multimodal composing. *TESOL Quarterly*, *54*(4), 954–979. https://doi.org/10.1002/tesq.566

Lave, J., & Wenger, E. (1991). *Situated learning: Legitimate peripheral participation*. Cambridge University. https://doi.org/10.1017/CBO9780511815355

Marrero-Colón, M. (2021). Translanguaging: Theory, concept, practice, stance … or all of the above. *Center for Applied Linguistics*. https://www.cal.org/resource-center/publications-products/translanguaging

Norton, B. (2001). Nonparticipation, imagined communities, and the language classroom. In M. Breen (Ed.), *Learner contributions to language learning: New directions in research* (pp. 159–171). Pearson Education.

Pentón Herrera, L. J. (2019). Advocating for Indigenous Hispanic EL students: Promoting the Indigenismo within. In H. A. Linville & J. Whiting (Eds.), *Advocacy in English language teaching and learning* (pp. 161–174). Routledge.

Vinogradova, P. (2011). *Digital storytelling in ESL instruction: Identity negotiation through a pedagogy of multiliteracies*. (Unpublished doctoral dissertation). University of Maryland Baltimore County, Baltimore, MD.

Vinogradova, P., Linville, H. L., & Bickel, B. (2011). "Listen to my story and you will know me": Digital stories as student-centered collaborative projects. *TESOL Journal*, *2*(2), 173–202. https://doi.org/10.5054/tj.2011.250380

Wenger, E. (1998). *Communities of practice: Learning, meaning, and identity*. Cambridge. https://doi.org/10.1017/CBO9780511803932

10 Presenting and Sharing Digital Stories

We love this final stage of the digital storytelling process. It is the time to "roll out the red carpet," pop some popcorn, and create an environment of celebration as MLs share their digital stories with each other. In our experience, this stage is usually joyful and full of applause and congratulations as MLs experience each other's stories. Even if they have peer edited and viewed parts of many of the digital stories as they were being created, there is something different and exciting about having them shared on a large screen in front of the whole class. In this chapter we discuss benefits and drawbacks of the various options for sharing ML digital stories. We also offer guidance on obtaining informed consent before sharing digital stories with others in the school or beyond, such as on school or teacher websites. Finally, we share ideas for digital storytelling showcases for your school and community audiences.

In-class Presentations

We consider in-class presentations of digital stories an essential part of the digital storytelling process. The in-class presentation ensures MLs have a real audience for their work, peers who have just gone through the same creative and collaborative process that they have. This in-class sharing also ensures a safe and familiar space where their digital stories are seen and heard. We suggest creating a festive atmosphere for viewing the digital stories. If your school has an auditorium or another room where events usually happen, consider reserving that space for the digital story presentations. For older MLs, you can also ask them how they want the in-class presentations to take place. They will likely have their own ideas of how to celebrate.

What if you have MLs who do not want their classmates or you to see their story?

We suggest making it clear from the beginning of the digital storytelling project that the last stage of the process is sharing digital stories with the class. Also be sure to let your MLs know that they will

DOI: 10.4324/9781003295730-12

not be required to share their digital story with anyone else. You may want to talk more with reticent MLs about making choices so they can feel comfortable sharing their digital story. As they create their digital story, they can purposefully not put anything in that they would not want to share. You may also have the most reticent MLs share last to build up their courage as they see others sharing.

As you have been involved in the digital stories throughout the creation process, you will already have a strong sense of each one. However, before this final step, be sure to preview each digital story before they are shown to the class. Depending on the stories, you might give a statement to the class before showing any of the digital stories, reminding the students of the personal nature of these digital stories and the need to respect each other's experiences and forms of expression. Some digital stories might recall traumatic events or have content that might be culturally sensitive or difficult for some students. While digital stories cannot and should not be censored (unless the topic or content is harmful or discriminatory), we need to create safe conditions for everyone to watch and process. For that you may want to prepare specific statements, such as a trigger warning, before particular stories in the case of deeply personal content or the recounting of traumatic events. You might also have a conversation with the whole class about personal expression and a respectful environment. Having previewed the digital stories first allows you to best prepare your MLs to view each of their classmates' digital stories openly and in a way that allows them to feel safe.

What if while watching students' final digital stories I realize that a story includes content that can be potentially offensive or violates principles of diversity, equity, and inclusion?

We have never encountered a situation like this but have talked at length about this possibility and how we would handle it. First of all, this question shows how important it is to have a conversation with MLs about appropriate topics and content and about the role of audience and setting for digital story viewing. It also shows how important it is for teachers to know what topics MLs are selecting for their digital stories and to be present throughout the production process to offer feedback, guide, ask questions, and clarify. In this case, we don't encourage vetoing topics or censoring content. Rather, we see further learning opportunities for MLs in having conversations about acceptance, inclusivity, and sensitivity to the experiences of others.

You also need to prepare your MLs to be good audience members. As this is a day of celebration, we recommend having audience members, including you as the teacher, give oral or written feedback, but not grade or otherwise evaluate each story. Think about a movie premier; it is usually full of praise, not critique. We take the same approach here. To prepare for peer feedback, MLs can engage in an activity to plan questions for each other and phrases to offer feedback. The class can also have a broader discussion of what makes a good digital story that can inform and frame their upcoming viewing. Remind your class beforehand of your expectations for audience members, aligned with the cultural expectations of your school location. Also remind MLs that everyone has done their best and that each digital story is a unique, valuable creation from the individuals in the class. (Please return to Chapter 9 for other suggestions for peer feedback.) You may also want to prepare family members that the in-class presentation of digital stories is happening in case MLs have an emotional response to sharing their own story or seeing another. Forewarning families that this can be a joyous but also emotional day can be helpful in ensuring your MLs get all the support they need. Here are a few more suggestions to make your digital storytelling share day a success:

- Do not invite others for the presentations. MLs have created their digital stories in a safe space and are being vulnerable with each other and you by sharing their digital stories. It is important that everyone in that space be a story creator and also sharing.
- Consider the order of the digital stories you share. More serious digital stories can be interwoven with more playful or funny digital stories to avoid audience fatigue.
- Be sure you take frequent breaks. Even though each digital story is short, it can be tiring watching multiple digital stories one after another.
- Check the timing carefully. If you do not have time to show all the digital stories in one class period, let MLs know beforehand whose story will be shown each day.
- Ensure the technology will work for each digital story. We suggest uploading them all to the same online location. Google Drive and YouTube (with privacy features on) are sites with large capacity for files so you can share the digital stories one by one without having to switch sites or enter passwords between stories.

What if my administrator wants to join in the sharing of stories?

In this case, we suggest talking to your administrator about the community of trust you have developed and encouraging the administrator to not come to the first viewing. You may have to have the first viewing in your classroom to ensure the safe space. After the first viewing, you may talk to your MLs and see if they are comfortable sharing with other school or community audiences.

School Presentations

While presentations of digital stories outside of your class are optional, we encourage you to organize a school- or program-wide event where the digital stories can be seen and appreciated by a wider audience after sharing them in class. Digital story viewing can also be integrated into an end-of-semester, term, or school-year celebration and can occur regularly, creating a new program tradition. You may use a movie theme or an awards night, even having the "directors" walk the red carpet, as Castañeda (2013) did in her project with high school MLs. We suggest that the MLs who produced the digital stories be invited but not required to participate in this event. In our experience, MLs are usually eager to share their work with others and get particularly excited after their digital stories are viewed and positively received in class. But not all MLs might be comfortable with a school-wide viewing and might prefer to be in the audience rather than in a spotlight. It is fine to give them this space.

For the school-wide event, consider the possibility of encouraging MLs to invite their families and friends. This is a moment of pride for MLs, and many want to share their digital stories with people close to them. In an event like this, MLs can be asked to introduce their digital stories and say a few words about their work. Here, comments and feedback from the audience, aside from applause and cheer, are not necessary as the point is to showcase digital stories and celebrate the producers. This is also a good time for the school or program administrator to attend and offer praise and words of encouragement.

What if my technology breaks down and I just can't get the stories to play?

This has happened to us of course, and to anyone else who has ever worked with technology! It is fine to use a laptop or a tablet and share the digital stories on the small screen with MLs gathered around during in-class presentations. For larger presentations, we also suggest always having a backup plan so you are able to present the digital stories another way, or an alternative activity to delay the presentations for a few minutes until you can figure out the technological glitches. Having your school technology expert or a friend who knows about technology standing by is also a good idea!

Community Presentations

As you have seen in many of the featured digital storytelling projects in this book, teachers often want to share MLs' digital stories with audiences beyond the school. The advantages of doing so are many. Community members become more aware of MLs in the schools and develop a greater understanding of and empathy for their backgrounds and strengths. In addition, MLs engage in self-advocacy by strategically telling and sharing their stories publicly (see Martin-Beltrán et al., 2020).

As a TESOL educator in a less linguistically diverse part of the US, Heather created the digital storytelling project, "We Live in La Crosse: Stories of Belonging" (WLLC), as a way to share stories of linguistically diverse individuals with the whole community. MLs ages 12 to over 50 from her region attended a free weeklong digital storytelling workshop that Heather and Polina co-facilitated in the summer of 2022. Then, Heather shared the stories with different audiences in the community at public presentations, including at the public library, university events, and middle schools and high schools. At each showing, the audiences enjoyed watching the stories and then answered post-viewing questions to share their reactions. Audience members who identify as culturally, linguistically, and/or ethnically diverse or whose ancestors are not from La Crosse, indicated they especially appreciated hearing about others who have struggled with a sense of belonging in their community. MLs who were not a part of the project also connected with the digital stories. A teacher at one of the middle schools reported that a few of the MLs who saw the digital stories felt seen and heard for the first time in their schools. It is through the sharing of stories that we connect with others and digital stories are a great way to do that.

Many of the digital stories created in the WLLC project are available at https://www.uwlax.edu/educational-studies/tesol-stories/#tm-digital-storytelling. Read more about this project in the featured digital storytelling project at the end of Chapter 11.

From this experience, we offer some advice for community presentations of digital stories. First, it is important to get buy-in and support from the various language groups that your MLs represent. Those groups can help you market your sharing event and may also want to work with you to create more stories raising awareness of their group in the community. Second, you will want to make sure you have obtained permission to share the digital stories publicly. We say more about this in the next section. Any community event is enhanced with food, so consider how you can make the event more enjoyable for audiences. You may also want to consider discussion sessions, time for questions and comments, or even guiding the viewing of each digital story so that audience members can understand each one in the best way. Finally, consider if you want audiences to have access to watch the digital stories after the event.

Sharing Digital Stories Online

After viewing digital stories in class and with broader audiences comes the question of making digital stories available online for general viewing. Teachers and programs might want to showcase the work of their MLs as well as show the innovative work they do themselves. For example, the Family Place Public Charter School created a separate space on their website to showcase digital stories developed by the MLs in Debora Amindani's and Carlye Stevens's classes https://www.thefamilyplacedc.org/digitalstorytellingeslclass (see featured digital storytelling project in Chapter 5). For us, the purpose of sharing is to offer the platform for ML voices as well as to offer digital stories as an educational resource to anyone interested. It is also an easy way for MLs to share their work with others.

Various considerations are involved when sharing digital stories online, including which online platform to use, how to preserve ML privacy, and how to select digital stories to share. We have posted our MLs' digital stories on the websites of the universities where we work (https://www.uwlax.edu/educational-studies/tesol-stories/#tm-221757 and https://www.american.edu/cas/tesol/student-projects.cfm#digital-storytelling-projects). Other teachers and many MLs upload digital stories to YouTube as well. Teachers can also set up their own website, for example using Google Sites, and upload the digital stories there through Google Drive. What is important is that all digital stories should be shared with the written permission of MLs, and their parents if the MLs are under the age of 18. We discuss this in more detail in the next section. As to selecting which digital stories to share, we have always asked MLs if they wanted their digital stories to be available online. It is up to them to decide. Some might be hesitant and worried about public attention and privacy while others can be enthusiastic and eager to share their digital stories online. We find it very important to let MLs know that sharing stories online is up to them, and we will respect their decision. As always, ML safety and security is our top priority. We additionally suggest the following to ensure to a greater degree that your MLs are safe when sharing digital stories online:

1. Consider modifying the digital stories so they do not contain MLs' full names. You can ask MLs if they want only their first name on their digital stories. The more anonymity online, the better.
2. Disable any commenting feature so audiences cannot leave comments on the digital story. This will avoid MLs having to see negative comments about their work, if there are any.
3. Disable any sharing feature. Do not allow anyone else to share the digital stories you post online. You do not want a digital story that you have shared to go viral.
4. Do allow MLs to share their own digital stories. It is fine if it goes viral this way.

Permission and Sharing Stories

We have mentioned previously that it is necessary to have permission to share MLs' digital stories beyond your classroom. What this permission entails will depend on your teaching environment and your MLs. Our best advice here is to find out what the process is at your school for sharing MLs' or other students' work. Some institutions may be very strict and not even allow student work to be shared beyond the school or online. Others may have very detailed processes to do so, involving the signature of the ML and their parent or guardian. Here we provide details of how you would typically need to get permission in US teaching contexts. Please be sure to consult administrators in your specific school to ensure you have followed the correct procedure.

If you work in a K-12 public school, parents are often asked to sign an agreement with the district for pictures of their children at school or at school events to be shared in marketing and publicity online and in paper formats. It is possible that the agreement extends to ML work. You should be able to find out from your district office a) if that agreement exists, b) what it entails, and c) which parents did not sign. Knowing this information will help you get specific permission to share MLs' digital stories in person or online with people outside of the school system. For MLs younger than 18 years of age, it is important to get their permission and their parents' or guardians' permission to share their digital stories. You might use a waiver like the example we provide. We recommend translating the document into all the languages your ML parents speak to ensure their understanding.

Video waiver example: Release of rights to media

I, ______________________________, hereby give, grant, assign and transfer, forever to the (school name) as a donation all my rights, title and interest in and to the digital story made by me on (day/month/year) and any written summaries or copies thereof and any documentation accompanying the recordings, for use by said School in any lawful way including publication in print or on the internet and video/audio production, except for the conditions specified below, if any:

Signature: ______________________________
Address: ______________________________
Date: ______________________________

Signature of School Representative: ______________________________

If you work in a university setting, we suggest reaching out to your Institutional Review Board (IRB) office. They will be able to tell you what type of permission you need to obtain and will likely give you a document you can use. Here is an example of an informed consent document from Heather's IRB office.

IRB informed consent example

Protocol Title: "We Live in La Crosse: Stories of Belonging"
Principal Investigator: Heather Linville, University of Wisconsin, La Crosse

Purpose

The purpose of this study is to research digital storytelling in language teaching and as a tool for sharing stories for community building in culturally and linguistically diverse communities. If you agree to participate in the second part of this research project, you will share your digital story with classmates at your school, community events, online at the UWL TESOL webpage (www.uwlax.edu/tesol), and at research conferences. You will have the opportunity to participate in the sharing of your story when possible but do not have to attend any presentation or event.

Potential Risks

This second part of the research project involves some risk. Sharing your digital story at your school and community events and research conferences, and having it posted online could mean that someone could link interview answers to you. It is also possible that someone could respond negatively to your story. You can reduce this risk by using a pseudonym or shortening your name when you share your story, having another person record your narrative, and not using identifying images. The researcher will not share negative responses publicly or with you, and not in response to any particular story. If you feel uncomfortable at any time, you can withdraw your participation from this second part of the research project.

Rights and Confidentiality

Participation in this part of the research project is voluntary and is not a required part of your course. You do not have to participate in this part of the research project. If you do not, you can still take the digital storytelling workshop and create a digital story. You can also share your story with anyone you choose to share it with. Your grade will not be impacted by participating or not in this part of the research study. You can withdraw from this study at any time, for any reason, and without penalty.

Possible Benefits

There is no cost nor any compensation to participate in this part of the research study. However, by participating in this research project, you are benefiting the community by helping others understand and reflect upon their beliefs about language learning and multilingualism. You may also benefit from the pride of creation by having your story shared.

If you have any questions about this survey or the research project, you can contact Dr. Heather Linville at hlinville@uwlax.edu or 608-785-8326. Questions regarding the protection of human subjects may be addressed to irb@uwlax.edu.

I give my informed consent to share my digital story at middle and high school viewing sessions, community events, research conferences, and on the UWL TESOL webpage (www.uwlax.edu/tesol).

Participant Name (please print) ____________________

Participant Signature ______________ Date______________

Researcher Signature ______________ Date______________

As stated at the beginning of the chapter, we believe this stage of digital storytelling is the most exciting and gratifying as a teacher. It is also the moment when MLs can feel the most proud of their creation. By preparing them well, ensuring their safety, and getting the appropriate permission, sharing their work will be as enjoyable and exciting as it can be!

In the following featured digital storytelling project, Aimee Leisy shares the challenges and joys of sharing MLs' digital stories at a public event. She also outlines how she prepares and supports MLs in sharing, and how they build confidence and connections on campus through the event.

In Part II, we have explored every stage in the process of creating a digital story. We hope you feel well prepared to start your own project with your MLs. In Part III, we return to more theoretical questions for digital storytelling projects. In the next chapter, we explore evaluation and assessment of digital stories, a part of the digital storytelling process that is often challenging for teachers.

Featured digital storytelling project: That's my story—a public speaking event

Name: Aimee Leisy
Position: Assistant Teaching Professor, Intensive English Program, Department of English at Wichita State University
Project Location: Wichita, Kansas, USA

> About one month ago, I came here. I was working in Japan as a high school teacher, but I was not confident of my teaching skill, so I wanted to go study abroad. And, second reason, I belonged to cheerleading squad when I was at my university. The name of this team is Shockers! It's the same name as WSU team.
>
> [International student digital storyteller]

I created "That's My Story," a public speaking event (Figure 10.1), as a way to champion the stories of international students on campus,

Figure 10.1 Student presenting his digital story in the "That's My Story" project. Photograph by Aimee Leisy.

especially the stories of the most recent arrivals who are studying English in preparation for academic courses. I wanted to boost the confidence of English learners and to share their linguistic and cultural diversity on campus. Having learned much about hobbies, experiences, and traditions of international students in my intensive English classes, I was sure their stories would appeal to others on campus. I previously wrote about this project in Leisy (2018).

This storytelling project is a cross-cutting curricular unit in the advanced level intensive English courses. In writing classes, the students review nonfiction narrative writing and write a first draft of their narrative. Meanwhile, in the speaking and listening classes, students prepare to present stories of cultural adjustment. At the beginning of the unit, students discuss their reactions to video recordings of stories from prior years. Next, we introduce the theme and learners follow the typical digital storytelling production process: imagining a story, receiving feedback from classmates, writing a narrative, collecting images, and storyboarding in PowerPoint (Vinogradova et al., 2011). We encourage students to use their first languages in the process, especially while researching or contacting relatives back home about their stories. For example, we observed students from Vietnam discuss content and elements of their digital stories in Vietnamese.

The final step in the project is to present before a live audience. To lower public speaking anxiety, we have dress rehearsals and offer encouraging feedback. For example, in 2018 a communications manager from the International Office gave public speaking tips for using a microphone and offered feedback to each student on their presentations. Speakers, including shy ones, have reported positive reactions to the experience of speaking before a large audience for the first time.

In January 2017, I coordinated the first storytelling event for the whole Intensive English program and advertised it in the online university newsletter. Intensive English faculty, current and former Intensive English students, and a large number of staff from the international center on campus came to support the speakers. After this event, the Office of International Education invited me to host "That's My Story" during International Education Week. Audience enjoyment and responsiveness at the live event encourages the storytellers and nurtures a sense of connection between them. It was especially moving to me to see two domestic first-year seminar students nodding and smiling as they listened to a student from Kuwait share his passion for Mustangs and knowledge of mechanics at the 2022 "That's My Story" event. Digital storytelling serves as a meaningful space to acquire cultural understanding. I hope other language educators will consider hosting live storytelling events to raise the unique voices of multilinguals. (Student stories are available at https://www.wichita.edu/admissions/international/intensive_english/studentstories.php).

References

Leisy, A. (2018, March). That's my story: ELLs share tales of cultural adjustment. *The Newsletter for Intercultural Communication Interest Section, TESOL*. http://newsmanager.commpartners.com/tesolicis/issues/2018-03-02/3.html

Vinogradova, P., Linville, H., & Bickel, B. (2011). "Listen to my story and you will know me": Digital stories as student-centered collaborative projects. *TESOL Journal*, *2*(2), 173–202. https://doi.org/10.5054/tj.2011.250380

References

Castañeda, M. (2013). "I am proud that I did it and it's a piece of me": Digital storytelling in the foreign language classroom. *CALICO Journal*, *30*(1), 44–62. https://doi.org/10.11139/cj.30.1.44-62

Martin-Beltrán, M., Montoya-Avila, A., & García, A. A. (2020). Becoming advocates: Positioning immigrant youth to share, connect, and apply their stories as tools for social change. *TESOL Journal*, *11*(4), 1–20. https://doi.org/10.1002/tesj.567

Part III Reflecting on Teaching and Learning through Digital Storytelling

11 Assessment and Evaluation in Digital Storytelling

Anytime we talk about digital storytelling, we always get questions about how we grade, or assess, students' digital stories. Assessment is a very important part of language teaching and learning and is certainly an important part of digital storytelling within a language classroom. Incorporating digital storytelling into our teaching, and planning our teaching using this engaging, creative, and collaborative narrative genre, has challenged us to rethink and redefine our approach to assessment in language classes. In this chapter, we present ways to traditionally assess MLs' digital stories relative to a variety of learning objectives, including language learning. We also present a rationale for adopting the ungrading approach to assessment of digital stories, as we have, and how that might make the most sense for you as well. Finally, we explore how you can evaluate your own digital storytelling projects and hopefully make them successful for the long term!

Principled Assessment of Digital Stories

As we all know, assessment is an important part of any teaching and learning environment and should therefore be carried out in a principled way. By doing so, we ensure that the information we have about MLs' language learning, which we give to them, their parents, and administrators in our teaching context, is as accurate as it can be. The five principles of assessment, as outlined by Brown and Abeywickrama (2010), are as follows:

- Validity—Does the assessment measure what it is supposed to measure? Do MLs feel the assessment measures their learning?
- Reliability—Does the assessment give the same result across situations and similar students? Do scorers of an assessment give similar scores to similar MLs?
- Authenticity—Is the assessment an authentic (i.e., real life) use of the skill? Would MLs use the skill being assessed in similar ways outside the classroom?

DOI: 10.4324/9781003295730-14

- Practicality—Is the assessment easily administered, including scoring, for the teacher? Is it cost effective?
- Washback—Is the impact of the assessment positive or negative for MLs?

While no assessment can meet all of these principles to a high degree, they offer an important place to start when thinking about assessing digital storytelling projects.

Is Our Assessment of Digital Stories Valid?

Arguably, the most important assessment principle is validity. If the assessment doesn't measure what it is supposed to, there is no point in doing the assessment. With digital storytelling, we must ask ourselves, what do we want to measure (and thus assess) of our MLs' digital storytelling skills? To answer this question, we suggest here that you return to Chapter 4, at which point you determined the learning goals you have for your MLs' digital storytelling work. MLs will likely have already achieved some of your learning objectives in the process of making their digital story, such as brainstorming thoughts and ideas, creating an outline, engaging in peer feedback, and selecting and using technological tools for digital story creation. Therefore, the assessment of those objectives is not necessary at this point; we assume they have achieved them since they have completed their digital story. Rather, at this point, we want to focus on the larger goal of creating a digital story, or stated as a learning objective, *Students will be able to compose a multimodal personal narrative*. Assessing this learning objective through the creation of a digital story is valid because the digital story is a multimodal personal narrative.

Is Our Assessment of Digital Stories Reliable?

Our next challenge, and the next most important assessment principle, is reliability. How do we reliably assess to what degree MLs have met the learning objective? In our example, we need to reliably assess to what degree MLs have been able to compose a multimodal personal narrative. There are at least three skill areas involved in the achievement of this objective, with many sub-skills, such as:

- Narrative skills—quality of writing, organization, use and control (accuracy) of language(s), complexity of language(s), appropriateness, comprehensibility, awareness of audience;
- Multimodal skills—use of three elements (voice, images, music), how elements work together, creativity, awareness of audience, translanguaging; and
- Technological skills—title and conclusion slides, clarity of images, transitions between images, use of subtitles, volume of voice and music.

Table 11.1 Sample analytic rubric for digital storytelling assessment (adapted from Vinogradova, 2014)

	An excellent digital story …	*A good digital story …*	*A satisfactory digital story …*	*A digital story that needs improvement …*
Purpose (10%)	Establishes a purpose early on and maintains a clear focus throughout. It is clear that the authors care about their DS and feel that they have something important to communicate.	Establishes a purpose early on and maintains focus through most of the digital story.	There are a few lapses in focus, but the purpose is fairly clear throughout the digital story.	It is difficult to figure out the purpose of the digital story.
Audience (10%)	Demonstrates strong awareness of audience. MLs can clearly explain how the audio, images, and music chosen fit the target audience.	Demonstrates good awareness of audience. MLs can partially explain how the audio, images, and music chosen fit the target audience.	Demonstrates some awareness of audience in the design. MLs find it difficult to explain how the audio, images, and music chosen fit the target audience.	Demonstrates limited awareness of the target audience. MLs cannot explain how the audio, images, and music fit the target audience.
Dramatic Question (10%)	Has content which is engaging. Audience is left with thought-provoking ideas and/or the digital story develops in a way that's different from initial expectations. Is useful for prompting discussion and dialogue.	Has content that is interesting. Audience is left with thought-provoking ideas and/or the story develops in a way that's different from initial expectations.	Has some surprises and/or insights, but digital story barely differs from the expectation.	Is predictable and not very interesting. Realization and expectation do not differ.

(*Continued*)

Table 11.1 (Continued)

	An excellent digital story …	*A good digital story …*	*A satisfactory digital story …*	*A digital story that needs improvement …*
Narrative (15%)	Is compelling and well written with concise use of words to make important points. It has accurate and appropriate use of language.	Is well written and makes important points. It has mostly accurate and appropriate use of language.	Is adequately written, but sometimes meanders or is confusing. Multiple inaccuracies make the message difficult to understand.	Is difficult to understand the point. It has inappropriate use of language.
Audio (15%)	Has voice quality that is clear and consistently audible throughout the digital story. Music enhances the digital story and matches the story line.	Has voice quality that is clear and consistently audible throughout the majority of the digital story. Music matches the story line.	Has voice quality that is clear and consistently audible throughout some of the digital story. Music matches the story line.	Has voice quality that needs more attention. Music is distracting, too loud, and/or inappropriate for the digital story line.
Pacing (10%)	Uses a pace (rhythm and voice punctuation) that fits the story line and helps the audience really engage with the story.	Uses a pace that is occasionally too fast or too slow for the digital story line. The pacing (rhythm and voice punctuation) is relatively engaging for the audience.	Uses a pace that often noticeably does not fit the digital story line. Audience is not consistently engaged.	Has no attempt to match the pace of the storytelling to the digital story line or the audience.
Emotion (10%)	Emotional dimension of the piece matches the story line well. Viewers are encouraged to care about the topic.	Emotional dimension of the piece somewhat matches the story line.	Emotional dimension of the piece is distracting (over the top) and/or does not add much to the story.	Emotional dimension of the piece is inappropriate OR absent.

Images (15%)	Has images that create a distinct atmosphere or tone that matches different parts of the story. The images communicate symbolism and/or metaphors. The meaning of the digital story is transformed by the use of images.	Has images that create a tone or atmosphere that matches some parts of the story. Images communicate symbolism and/or metaphors. The digital story relies on images to convey meaning.	Has images that attempt to create a tone or atmosphere but needs more work. Image choice is logical. Images are decorative; the digital story is not altered by the use of images.	Shows little or no attempt to use images to create an appropriate tone or atmosphere. Images interfere or are at cross-purposes with the digital story's meaning.
Credits (5%)	All people, organizations, quotes, ideas, music, and contributors are appropriately credited. Permission has been obtained (or Creative Commons license information provided) for images and audio not created by the author.	Most people, organizations, quotes, ideas, music, and contributors are appropriately credited. Permission has been obtained (or Creative Commons license information provided) for images and audio not created by the author.	Some people, organizations, quotes, ideas, music, and contributors are appropriately credited. Permission has been obtained (or Creative Commons license information provided) for images and audio not created by the author.	Very few or no people, organizations, quotes, or contributors are credited appropriately.

You can see that some of these skills are not easily defined. For example, creativity and how the multimodal elements work together are subjective and thus difficult to assess. There are also varying degrees of achievement for many of the skills, from very well done to barely meeting the objective. Therefore, to reliably assess the objective, we need to clearly define what we expect in each skill area and the levels of achievement for each. We suggest using an analytic rubric to assess each skill area, as in Table 11.1, or a holistic rubric to assess the entire digital story. Here we offer an example of an analytic rubric which combines all skill areas, albeit with different terminology. This rubric was informed by the elements of digital storytelling from Lambert (2006), which we introduced in Chapter 2.

> View again the video recorded at UMBC in 2009 and focus on the sections where Heather and others talk about assessing digital stories, especially with rubrics: https://www.youtube.com/watch?v=72aJ1G0acSE&t=9s.

Even with a well-designed rubric, it is very challenging to assess creative works. As Reed (2008) puts it, "No rubric can describe the magic" (p. 26). Indeed, in the preceding rubric, under the category *images*, the highest score includes the description, "The meaning of the story is transformed by the use of images." We remain unconvinced that we, as teachers, could assess in a trustworthy or reliable manner MLs' use of images and if their digital story was transformed by the images or not. Reed (2008) points to several challenges in this endeavor, including the fact that MLs come to us from different generational and cultural understandings of images and how they can and should be used. Personal preferences are also at play here, as in all creative endeavors. We also need to keep in mind that we are not teaching a class on photography, filmmaking, or multimodal composing. Rather we are guiding MLs to use digital multimodal composing in digital storytelling to facilitate language learning and translanguaging, offering creative space for MLs to express themselves and use their full linguistic and multimodal repertoires. We will return to this point later when we discuss the ungrading approach we prefer for evaluation of digital storytelling projects.

Is Our Assessment of Digital Stories Authentic and Practical?

Our next concerns in assessment are authenticity and practicality. Digital storytelling is a skill that can be used outside of the classroom in "real life," such as when MLs create videos to share on social media. It is also a way for them to talk about themselves, their lives, and important aspects or events. Therefore, assessing language use, translanguaging, and digital media skills can be done authentically through digital stories. However, the assessment of digital stories might not be considered very practical because using a detailed rubric to score each digital story will take quite a bit of time. As in all assessments, there are trade-offs; no assessment will meet all the five principles well. In this case, if you assess your MLs' digital stories using a rubric, you will likely have to spend more time on assessment, making it less practical. The ungrading approach we discuss later also addresses challenges with the principle of practicality.

Is Our Assessment of Digital Stories Providing Students with Positive Washback?

The final assessment principle to consider is washback. Ideally, assessing MLs leads to greater learning and increased motivation to learn and do better in the future. One way to guarantee that is to have an assessment as principled as possible, as we've discussed earlier. It is also essential to provide useful feedback to MLs in a timely manner. For digital stories, the feedback can be in the form of a rubric score, but we suggest you also give narrative comments. Positive washback can also occur as MLs give feedback to each other if well prepared to do so (as discussed in Chapter 9). Self-assessment is another good way to ensure positive washback, having MLs reflect on how well they did in achieving the objective(s) of the digital story.

Ungrading Digital Stories

We have so far demonstrated how digital storytelling can be assessed. Now we turn our thoughts to a different approach to grading that we suggest for digital storytelling projects: *ungrading*. Ungrading is an approach to assessment in which ML self-assessment and teacher feedback take the place of formal grading and assigned points or letter grades are avoided or minimized. This approach has become more popular recently and has been in use in educational contexts from elementary schools to universities, and in education of all subjects worldwide for many decades. The main reason for this approach is to avoid the negative washback from assessments that MLs often experience as they work hard and feel great stress to achieve a high grade and the success that comes with it. Ungrading also aims to focus MLs on their learning rather than a grade, hopefully motivating them to learn more. In one language teaching example, Armstrong (2010) found that grading made no difference in target language accuracy or complexity in writing essays. As she points out, "We do not normally write for the purpose of evaluation but for communication. Providing students with opportunities to communicate that reward experimentation and risk-taking may actually benefit the student in the long run" (Armstrong, 2010, p. 699). We believe that the communicative purpose of digital storytelling, sharing stories among classmates and other audiences, makes it an authentic task that does not require or need grading.

For these reasons, we have embraced ungrading as the assessment approach to our own digital storytelling projects. For us, the potential negative washback from assessing MLs' digital stories, the lack of reliability, and the fact that there is no way to accurately assess multimodal composing is too high a price to pay. Assessment should support MLs' creativity, multimodal choices, and forms of expression. We are not judges of creativity, but rather are educators who introduce MLs to this genre of expression and create space for their multimodal, multilingual, and personal language learning.

We are, however, very purposeful in our ungrading. We give feedback and input at every stage of digital story production, scaffolding MLs through the process. We make sure our MLs always have clear deadlines for the completion of each stage. In this way, we know what we expect from MLs and MLs know what we expect from them. We mark their performance at each stage as *complete*, *partially complete*, or *incomplete*, and offer targeted feedback that does not overwhelm MLs or their creative process. In this way, our "assessment" is a useful part of project scaffolding and an opportunity for the MLs to reflect on their own work, as we, language educators, gain a better understanding of how the project is going and how the MLs are progressing in their learning. See Table 11.2 for an example of a checklist that can be used in lieu of grading. Completion indicates that the ML has met the objectives of the project and has received full credit.

An important part of the ungrading process is ML self-assessment, which contributes to the overall evaluation of the digital storytelling process for each ML. Self-assessment can be conducted in a variety of ways, such as in a face-to-face conference, in writing, or as a self-recorded reflection. The self-assessment can also be conducted in any language or with translanguaging so MLs can use their whole linguistic repertoire to fully reflect upon and express their learning. In the following, we provide sample questions that MLs can reflect upon in their self-assessment. The students can be asked to reflect upon the following questions and include their responses, in any language, in a 400–600 word self-assessment of their digital stories.

1. What was your digital story about? Why did you choose that topic or focus? What ideas or concepts did it help you explore? Given the chance, would you choose the same topic or focus again?
2. How did you use your language(s) in your digital story? How did the audience figure into your decision making about language usage? How would you use language(s) differently in a future digital story?
3. Why did you choose the images you used in your digital story? In what ways did they help tell your story? How did your images help you connect with your audience?
4. How skillful did you feel with the video editing software? How well were you able to use transitions, modify volume of voice and music, include subtitles or other text on screen? Which technological skills do you want to keep working on?

Table 11.2 Sample digital storytelling process checklist for ungrading assessment

Stage	*Complete*	*Partially complete*	*Incomplete*	*Comments*
1. Pre-planning (watched and analyzed sample stories)				
2. Story circle				
3. Draft of narrative and peer review				
4. Collection of potential images and music				
5. Finalized narrative				
6. Storyboard and peer review				
7. Audio recording of narrative				
8. Uploading of elements to software				
9. Video editing and peer review				
10. Presentation of story to class and peer feedback				

5. Why did you choose the music you used in your digital story? In what ways did it help tell your story? How did your music help you connect with your audience?
6. Were you happy with how the audience responded to your story? Why or why not? In what ways do you think you could change your digital story to elicit a better audience response?
7. What did you learn from this project? What more would you like to learn related to digital storytelling?
8. How much did you enjoy this project? What could help you enjoy it more?

In our earlier work (see Vinogradova, 2014 and Vinogradova et al., 2011), we were curious to see how the MLs would respond to the ungrading approach to assessment and grading. We also wondered how the ungrading approach would impact their motivation. What we observed repeatedly in various classes, even when the MLs were not formally assessed or were not getting a grade that would count toward the overall grade for the class, was that the MLs were motivated by the project itself and worked very hard to complete it the best they could. MLs work hard on digital storytelling because they care and are interested in the project and want to share their digital stories with people outside of class, not for a grade.

Polina observed the same approach during digital storytelling work at the Family Place Public Charter School (see the featured digital storytelling project in Chapter 5). While the digital stories and all work accompanying their development were ungraded and happened during the last two weeks of the school year after high-stakes assessment was done, MLs were eager to participate, came to class, and attended optional office hours that one of the teachers held one Friday for extra support. As both instructors noted, the MLs were engaged and involved in class work more than during regular classes. Their performance was driven by interest in digital storytelling work, specifically by telling stories about their lives, rather than by grades.

We know that ungrading might sound scary to language educators and in some educational settings it can be very challenging or almost impossible to not grade. We hope that you are willing to experiment here and are empowered and reassured after seeing the results of your MLs' work when they are not thinking and worrying about grades but are engaged and working as they are enjoying the meaningful process of creating their own digital stories.

Focus on Language: Assessing Language Use through Digital Stories

We now turn to how digital storytelling can be used as an alternative assessment of MLs' language abilities. For many language educators, using digital storytelling projects is a creative way to have MLs practice and authentically use the target language. Alternative assessment, such as projects, portfolios, or checklists, is a common way to assess MLs that is considered more authentic and provides more positive washback to MLs than tests (Al-Mahrooqi & Denman, 2015). Digital storytelling is, itself, a form of alternative assessment and can be used to assess MLs' language use in an authentic way. One challenge to consider is translanguaging, especially if you want the digital storytelling project to assess MLs' translanguaging skills. If we think about the role of translanguaging in language learning, we realize that standardized and formal assessments (e.g., tests, quizzes, assessment of the use of grammar structures and vocabulary) are not sufficient as they usually do not allow MLs to translanguage. However, digital storytelling can authentically assess MLs' translanguaging skills.

Similar to our focus on assessing MLs' abilities to create digital stories in the previous section, here we will also analyze each principle of assessment with respect to language use, including translanguaging, in digital stories. Please keep in mind that in this section, unlike the previous, we are using digital stories as an alternative assessment (i.e., not a test or a quiz) to assess MLs' language skills.

Can Digital Stories Provide a Valid Assessment of Language Use?

A valid assessment is one that measures what it is supposed to measure. In the case of language use, an assessment could measure MLs' language skills related to the main skills of reading, writing, listening, and speaking as well as the additional language skills like grammar, vocabulary, and pronunciation. Assessments can also measure translanguaging skills related to the use of multiple languages. Here, it is important to think about how language is used in digital storytelling. MLs use their languages to write their narrative, to read out loud their narrative as they record it, and to write text on screen such as subtitles, the title slide, or credits at the end of the story. Therefore, digital storytelling can be a valid assessment of MLs' writing (including grammar and vocabulary) skills, pronunciation skills, and to a certain extent their reading skills. You may find it challenging to require translanguaging, depending on your MLs' linguistic repertoires and their comfort level in using their multiple languages. If you do not require translanguaging, however, then it will not be valid to assess it. Digital storytelling is also a valid assessment of pronunciation skills as MLs read their text out loud, but not of speaking skills. It would also not be a valid assessment of their listening skills, which do not come into play in the final digital story product. However, we should note that listening skills are practiced while digital stories are being produced. For example, MLs listen to each other, listen to their own recorded narratives and evaluate the quality, and engage in peer discussions at each stage of the digital storytelling process.

Can Digital Stories Provide a Reliable Assessment of Language Use?

To be reliable, we want to ensure that our assessment of language use in digital stories is consistent across MLs and time. The best way to ensure this is to use a rubric with very clear definitions of each level of language use for writing (as evidenced in the written narrative), reading and pronunciation of the narrative in the voiceover, and translanguaging. The expectations for each skill will vary depending on your MLs' language level. The following sample rubric (Table 11.3) is aimed for students at the intermediate to advanced level of language.

Table 11.3 Sample narrative rubric for digital storytelling with translanguaging

Criteria	*A digital story that meets expectations …*	*A digital story that approaches expectations …*	*A digital story that does not meet expectations …*
Organization	Has an engaging opener, a clear sequence of events, and a strong conclusion.	Has an engaging opener, a clear sequence of events, and/or a strong conclusion.	Has no or a weak opener, a confusing sequence of events, and no or a weak conclusion.
Content	Has enough details to follow without unrelated information; translanguaging enhances the meaning of the story.	Has enough details but some unrelated information; translanguaging supports the meaning of the story.	Has too many or too few details, impeding comprehension; translanguaging confuses the meaning of the story.
Grammar	Demonstrates correct use of verb tenses in complex sentences and translanguaging that is clear from context or explained in subtitles or text on screen.	Demonstrates understandable use of verb tenses in complex sentences and translanguaging that is clear from context or explained in subtitles or text on screen.	Demonstrates incorrect use of verb tenses or is overly reliant upon simple sentences; translanguaging is unclear and unexplained.
Expression	Uses vocabulary that accurately conveys emotion of story and a register that is appropriate for audience.	Uses vocabulary that conveys emotion of story and a register that is appropriate for audience.	Uses vocabulary that is too simple or limited to convey emotion of story and a register that is not appropriate for audience.

Can Digital Stories Provide an Authentic and Practical Assessment of Language Use?

Alternative assessments, in general, provide MLs more authentic ways to use their language(s), and digital storytelling as an alternative assessment is no different. In contrast to other forms of assessment that invent situations for MLs to pretend they are communicating, the primary purpose of the digital story is to communicate authentically with an audience. Thus, digital storytelling is an authentic assessment of the use of language(s). However, alternative assessments are often less practical than a test or quiz that can be graded quickly and, oftentimes, by a computer. Assessing use of language(s) through a digital story is more time consuming as it must be done one by one, viewing each story multiple times. We believe it is worth the additional effort, but practicality in assessment is a point to keep in mind when planning your digital storytelling project.

Can the Assessment of Language Use via Digital Stories Provide Positive Washback to MLs?

Positive washback from assessments is very important, especially for MLs who are beginning language learners or nontraditional MLs, such as migrant adults who have to learn new language features later in life. With proper attention paid to providing positive feedback along with any negative critiques, we believe MLs can experience positive washback from the assessment of language use in their digital story.

Evaluating Your Digital Storytelling Project

As with any pedagogical practice we undertake, it is also important to evaluate how effective the digital storytelling process itself was for you and for your MLs. Related to assessment of individual ML success in achieving your objectives, evaluation also takes into account how the project worked for the group of MLs as a whole and for you as a teacher. Many times, this evaluation is the feeling a teacher has at the end of a term or a project. Are you satisfied that your MLs learned a lot and did well? Or are you relieved

> After doing a digital storytelling project with university undergraduate pre-service teachers, Heather felt that the project was kind of a bust. The pre-service teachers' stories were fine but she didn't feel they enjoyed the project or got that much out of it. In order to understand more and evaluate the project, she read through the pre-service teachers' reflections on the project. In doing so, she got a completely different feeling for the project. Many pre-service teachers indicated that the project helped them get to know each other and bond as a class quickly at the beginning of the semester, something that doesn't happen in a typical undergraduate class. They also indicated all the ways they felt they could use digital storytelling in their own, future classrooms. The evaluation of the project, more than just how Heather felt about it, was very useful. Based on it, Heather now plans to keep doing digital stories in that teacher education course!

the project is over and feel MLs are, too? While these feelings are valid, we suggest you analyze a little deeper to truly understand and evaluate your digital storytelling project.

Here are some questions to help you evaluate and reflect on your own digital storytelling project:

1. How many MLs met the learning objective(s) of the project?
2. What else did MLs learn from the project, based on your assessment?
3. How many of the MLs indicated they enjoyed the project? (This information can come from MLs' self-assessment reflections or from discussions after showing the digital stories.)
4. What aspects of the project did MLs indicate they would like changed?
5. How did each step of the project go? Were some steps easier and some harder? How could you adjust the steps that were harder?
6. Did MLs find the project meaningful? In what ways?
7. Were you able to share the stories with other audiences (e.g., other classes at school)? Did those audiences find them meaningful?
8. What else do you need to know to better evaluate your digital storytelling project?

As we can see from Heather's example, getting feedback from MLs can be very informative for our project evaluation. For example, MLs can be asked to write a reflective paper following some guiding questions. Like Heather, Polina does this with her TESOL pre-service teachers. This has allowed her to improve the project experience for the pre-service teachers over the years. MLs can also be asked to complete a short survey which can be offered in MLs' home languages as well as in English. While survey answers might not provide details and deep reflections, they will convey overall mood and MLs' emotional response to the project. And some MLs might be willing and able to offer more details and thoughts on the project. Based on your evaluation, we hope you will find enough positive benefits to try your digital storytelling project again!

In the featured digital storytelling project in this chapter, Heather explores how she analyzed community beliefs related to multilingualism and migration through the sharing of MLs' digital stories in the project "We Live in La Crosse: Stories of Belonging." While she did not need to assess each digital story, as the participants were not in a graded class, she evaluated the project to determine how it could be improved for future iterations.

In the next and final chapter of this book, we return to some of the theoretical and foundational understandings that guide digital storytelling work for us. As we do so, we hope to answer any final questions you may have about digital storytelling and encourage you once more to try your own digital storytelling project, no matter what your teaching context.

Featured digital storytelling project: We live in La Crosse: Stories of belonging—a community engagement project

Name: Heather Linville
Position: Professor, University of Wisconsin, La Crosse
Project Location: La Crosse, WI, USA

As a TESOL educator in a less linguistically diverse part of the United States, I created the digital storytelling project "We Live in La Crosse: Stories of Belonging" (WLLC) as a way to share stories of linguistically diverse individuals with the whole community. I invited multilingual individuals (ages 12 and above) from the La Crosse region to attend a free, weeklong digital storytelling workshop in the summer of 2022. The goal was to have these multilingual individuals tell their stories and share them with others in La Crosse as a way to highlight different voices in our community. The workshop took place at one of the local middle schools and was funded by a grant from the Wisconsin Humanities Council. Dr. Polina Vinogradova (co-author of this book) co-facilitated the summer workshop with me. We had 11 participants, including two teacher assistants.

We introduced the workshop participants to digital storytelling by showing our own stories and some other examples. We introduced the main themes of the workshop (multilingualism, migration, and belonging) early on the first day. We were purposeful about including translanguaging from the beginning. For example, we had participants create multilingual name tags, showed multilingual digital stories as examples, and asked participants to answer survey questions about multilingualism and then discuss their beliefs. While not a requirement of the workshop, we hoped the participants would want to tell stories of how multilingualism and/or migration have impacted their lives, and their sense of belonging in La Crosse. In the end, all but two of the stories were about these topics.

The ML participants, through the creation of a digital story, benefitted from reflecting on their lives and community building from within. As one participant noted, the workshop "provides the chance to slow down, take their time to think about something, create something, based on what your interest is or what your life has been, or a hobby or something that is connected to each person." The workshop also created community among the participants, supporting empowerment of multilingual individuals in La Crosse. Participants noted that connecting with others who were multilingual was an additional positive outcome from the workshop.

Over the next few months, with funding from the La Crosse Community Foundation, I shared the digital stories for which I had permission with different audiences in the community, including at the public library, university events, and middle and high schools. At each showing, I felt the audiences enjoyed watching the stories, but I wanted to better understand the audience reactions. Therefore, I also asked audiences to answer questions in Google Forms after viewing each story. In this way, I was able to more accurately evaluate the project.

Based on audience responses, this community is open to migrants' and MLs' stories, and they tend to view La Crosse as a diverse place where all are welcome. Audience members commented on the importance of storytelling in our society to learn about and connect with others. This project was successful at critically engaging the community with questions of belonging and inclusion of MLs. Respondents felt very strongly that someone born in the United States, even if they have migrated to somewhere else, belongs in our community (86% of respondents). Respondents also felt, though less strongly, that someone who lives here, even if not born here, can belong (70% of respondents). Many referred to their own cultural heritage or migrant background, while others shared elements of culture that they enjoy from other countries, such as food, music, or sports. A few respondents seemed to insist that they were born in the United States and were thus "fully" American. However, these responses were minimal and represent less than 5% of the total.

In addition, anecdotally, one ESL teacher at one of the middle schools reported that a few of the MLs who saw the digital stories felt seen and heard for the first time in their schools. One teacher asked her seventh grade (about 12 or 13 years old) students to write thank you letters to me after I presented in her classes. These letters show that students who are not ethnically White or whose ancestors are not from La Crosse also appreciated hearing about others who have struggled with a sense of belonging in their community.

Through the evaluation of this digital storytelling project, I am able to understand better the impact of the MLs' digital stories in the community. I hope others will consider creating a community engagement project where digital stories created by MLs or others can be shared across the community. It is through the sharing of stories that we connect with others, and digital stories are a great way to do that. Many of the digital stories created in the WLLC project are available at https://www.uwlax.edu/educational-studies/tesol-stories/#tm-digital-storytelling.

References

Al-Mahrooqi, R., & Denman, C. (2015). Alternative assessment. *TESOL Encyclopedia*. Wiley.

Armstrong, K. M. (2010). Fluency, accuracy, and complexity in graded and ungraded writing. *Foreign Language Annals*, *43*(4), 690–702.

Brown, H. D., & Abeywickrama, P. (2010). *Language assessment: Principles and classroom practices*. Pearson Education, Inc.

Lambert, J. (2006). *Digital storytelling: Capturing lives, creating community* (2nd ed.). Digital Diner Press.

Reed, Y. (2008). No rubric can describe the magic: Multimodal designs and assessment challenges in a postgraduate course for English teachers. *English Teaching: Practice and Critique*, *7*(3), 26–41. https://files.eric.ed.gov/fulltext/EJ832215.pdf

Vinogradova, P. (2011). *Digital storytelling in ESL instruction: Identity negotiation through a pedagogy of multiliteracies*. (Unpublished doctoral dissertation). University of Maryland Baltimore County, Baltimore, MD.

Vinogradova, P. (2014). Digital stories in a language classroom: Engaging students through a meaningful multimodal task. *The FLTMAG*. https://fltmag.com/digital-stories/

Vinogradova, P., Linville, H. L., & Bickel, B. (2011). "Listen to my story and you will know me": Digital stories as student-centered collaborative projects. *TESOL Journal*, *2*(2), 173–202. https://doi.org/10.5054/tj.2011.250380

12 Revisiting the Big Picture

You have made it! We hope you either have already embarked upon your own digital storytelling process by now, or you are well into planning it. We also hope you will continue to revisit this guide as you undertake your future digital storytelling journeys. We began this book with a historical overview of digital storytelling, especially in language education. It is now your turn to add to this ongoing story as you and your MLs create your digital stories.

We hope this book has guided you well through the process of digital storytelling, helping you prepare, plan for, and incorporate a digital storytelling project with translanguaging into your language class. In this guide, we have aimed to:

1. Explain why and how digital storytelling is useful in language teaching,
2. Provide a clear, step-by-step process for creating digital stories in the language classroom,
3. Connect digital storytelling to the goals of translanguaging so it can be more easily understood and incorporated into language teaching, and
4. Provide multiple examples and resources to support digital storytelling creation with translanguaging in any language classroom.

Our stories in this guide about the many digital storytelling projects we have undertaken support our belief that it is a worthy pedagogical activity for any language classroom. First, digital storytelling supports language learning. Its collaborative nature encourages MLs to develop their critical language awareness as they negotiate for meaning and make decisions about language usage in their digital stories. Digital storytelling projects also provide opportunities for MLs to engage in storytelling and make connections with others in their language classrooms and beyond as they tell their own stories and listen to those of others. These connections deepen the relationships MLs have with you, with each other, and with their school community when their digital stories are shared. In this way, digital storytelling also provides an opportunity for you to create a community of

DOI: 10.4324/9781003295730-15

practice (CoP) in your classroom where each ML contributes to the CoP, sharing their strengths and getting support from others for areas that they are not as strong in. Digital storytelling is also a creative multimodal activity, an area lacking in many classrooms today, and empowering to MLs as they showcase their lifeworlds in various multimodal ways with complete creative control.

As we've demonstrated in this book, digital storytelling is also a useful vehicle to encourage and develop translanguaging. This is also an opportunity to connect with MLs' language heritage and utilize their full linguistic repertoires, as each step of the digital storytelling process engages MLs in understanding and improving their translanguaging skills. When preparing for a digital storytelling project, MLs can watch digital stories that are in various languages and use translanguaging. In the story circle, MLs can express themselves using their full linguistic repertoire. When drafting their digital story narrative, MLs can think about which aspects of their linguistic repertoire they want to use and the changes in the meaning of their stories as they use different language features. The storyboard is another opportunity for MLs to visualize language usage throughout their digital story. Peer feedback conversations can be multilingual throughout the process, as well as peer support conversations as MLs work on the detailed editing of their digital stories. And finally, multilingual conversations naturally take place as MLs view the digital stories created by their classmates and give feedback for each one.

In these ways, digital storytelling is a tool for social justice, especially linguistic social justice when combined with translanguaging. As digital stories created by MLs are shared, their authentic voices and experiences are shared as well. Audiences learn and understand more about MLs, language learning, and the linguistic diversity in their communities, hopefully creating more inclusive spaces for MLs. This is our final goal of this guide; that more teachers of MLs find ways to support translanguaging and to further the view that multilingualism is natural and desirable in our schools and society.

Along with the multiple benefits of digital storytelling, we also recognize the challenges. As teachers, we must assess our MLs' work and progress toward language learning goals. To meet this end, we encourage the use of digital stories as alternative assessments in language classrooms, a creative alternative to tests or quizzes that tend to decontextualize language use. However, we also understand that assessing a creative work is messy and hope that you will engage in digital storytelling projects in spite of these challenges. Perhaps one of your digital storytelling projects can be featured in a future edition of this book!

We would like to conclude this book by sharing one final featured digital storytelling project. In this project, Nadezda Pimenova shares how a large language program engages international MLs in the United States in digital storytelling to help them with their academic studies and to find a sense of belonging in their new community. It is a clear example of how digital storytelling supports social justice as MLs and their audience members learn to challenge stereotypes about being an international student.

Featured digital storytelling project: "Telling my Story": An EAP bridge course project

Name: Nadezda Pimenova
Position: Senior Lecturer at Purdue Language and Cultural Exchange (PLaCE), Purdue University
Project Location: West Lafayette, Indiana, USA

Every year, our English for Academic Purposes (EAP) program welcomes a cohort of some 400 incoming international students. Our EAP program collectively created the "Telling my Story" digital storytelling project as a capstone project for our students to reflect on their development during their first year of college, and as a way for students to share their stories with each other and the university community. In their digital stories, students tell a meaningful story connecting course concepts to their academic, cultural, language, personal, and/or social development. Students' stories have covered such topics as learning kung fu when studying online, how procrastination affected them during their first semester in college, and how they optimized energy management.

Throughout the semester, students learn about self-reflection, narratives, and digital storytelling. In my course, I start introducing students to digital storytelling by showing former students' stories and TED Talks such as "The Danger of a Single Story" by Chimamanda Adichie and "Embracing Otherness, Embracing Myself" by Thandiwe Newton. Students learn about reflective thinking and practice it when connecting these stories to their own experiences. We spend time talking about students' culture as well as cultural models and cross-cultural differences. When teaching new vocabulary and idioms, I often ask students to share if they had a similar expression in their language. By the end of the semester, students produce their stories. At the heart of each story is deep reflection, where students look inward for personal growth or change during their first semester at college. Many students tell stories about their sense of belonging in the university community. By reflecting on their experiences, many English language learners show their openness and appreciation of differences and the ability to compare their home culture with US cultural orientations.

To create their digital stories, I encourage students to use a slideshow app such as PowerPoint in the format of a Pecha Kucha 20x20 presentation (www.pechakucha.com). Pecha Kucha uses 20 slides or images shown for 20 seconds each with audio commentary by the presenter (either live or recorded). The Pecha Kucha format works well for a class project because it provides a clear structure to work with while leaving lots of room for individual creativity and expression (Bush et al., 2022). The Pecha Kucha format also breaks down a big presentation into smaller parts that are more manageable for students to complete.

I schedule presentations for the last day of class in a roundtable format or in front of the class. This digital storytelling project empowers students to communicate their perspectives to others. Digital storytelling provides a platform that works for learning at a personal level as well as for learning at a class, community, and institutional level because these stories can be shared through public presentations and online video hosting sites. Often, I invite guests to watch students' presentations, and their reactions have been positive. Audience members have shared that students' stories challenged stereotypes and overgeneralizations and helped them to transform their perceptions of what it means to be an international student.

Ideally, students' digital projects have a life beyond or outside our class. For instance, students can include their videos in the e-portfolio final project for a subsequent EAP course. I encourage instructors in other EAP programs to consider a digital storytelling project to showcase their international students. Some of the digital stories created in the "Telling My Story" project are available on my department YouTube channel https://www.youtube.com/@purduelanguageandculturale7591 as part of our Student Showcase.

References

Adichie, C. (2009, October 7). *The danger of a single story* [Video]. TED Talks, online at https://www.youtube.com/watch?v=D9Ihs241zeg

Bush, D. H., Allen, M., Farner, N., & Pimenova, N. (2022). Designing virtual learning spaces to promote language and cultural exchange. In M. Allen, E. Ene, & K. McIntosh (Eds.), *Internationalization at home: Second language perspectives on developing language and cultural exchange programs in higher education* (pp. 60–78). University of Michigan Press.

Newton, T. (2011, July 20). *Embracing otherness, embracing myself* [Video]. TED Talks, online at https://www.youtube.com/watch?v=uzKBGtf0i0M

Index

Pages in *italics* refer to figures and pages in **bold** refer to tables.